WERE YOU THERE?...

*See Jesus' cross and resurrection through
the eyes of those who were there*

Gerard Chrispin

DayOne

First Printed 2021

Printed by 4Edge

ISBN 978-1-84625-682-0

Published by Day One Publications

Ryelands Road, Leominster, HR6 8NZ

Telephone 01568 613 740 FAX 01568 611 473

email—sales@dayone.co.uk

web site—www.dayone.co.uk

Christian Prison Resourcing, (CPR), PO Box 61685, London, SE9 9BL—

www.cprministries.org.uk

Co-published with United Beach Missions/Christian Answer—

https://www.ubm.org.uk/christian-answer

Practical notice about 'Were You There?':

If you would like to participate in the Study Book/Correspondence Course or Discussion Course as an individual or as an organiser, please contact CPR at Christian Prison Resourcing, (CPR), PO Box 61685, London, SE9 9BL—www.cprministries.org.uk

Listen, chapter by chapter, to 'Were You There?' at info@thoughtfortheday.info Download complete audio of 'Were You There?' at info@thoughtfortheday.info Create your own audio CD from 'ISO' files.

Ready-made CDs are also available from the same address. Please ask for details from info@thoughtfortheday.info

This book is dedicated to those worldwide, and in our country, who suffer because they know the crucified and risen Lord, and live to seek to please Him, rather than go with the world.

It is also dedicated to Jemimah, who I pray will grow up to know the Lord Jesus Christ as the loving Saviour who died for her and rose to be her Lord.

ENDORSEMENTS

I've known and benefited greatly from Gerard Chrispin's ministry for over thirty years. The heart of what he has to say is the very heart of the Christian message—the cross of Christ. You will hear this coming through again and again in everything he says and writes. There's nothing more important anyone could say.

Dr Peter Williams, M.A. (Cantab) M.Phil (Cantab) Ph.D, Principal of Tyndale House, Cambridge

Contents

Foreword by Professor Stephen Taylor, Liverpool

B.Sc (ACGI), MEng, PhD, C.Eng, FIEE, FInstPhys, DSc (DIC)
Professor of Electrical Engineering and Electronics at University of Liverpool

The death and resurrection of the Lord Jesus Christ are the most significant events in all of history. The death was recorded both by the four biblical (Gospel) and secular authors and witnessed by the thousands (perhaps tens of thousands) who came into and out of Jerusalem on that day. This short book by Gerard Chrispin focuses on that most significant of events from the point of view of the various eyewitnesses, from those who were 'there'.

This book is a series of 'snapshots' of some of those people, both friends of Jesus and foes who were actually present at the cross or involved with Christ in some way on that eventful day. We meet the Roman governor Pilate who 'played politics' with the life of Jesus. We hear the taunts of the religious but godless rulers who, like many today, ridiculed Jesus. We are introduced to the released prisoner, Barabbas the murderer, reprieved because Jesus literally died in his place. We see the ugly face of human sin as we are told of the murderous mob who, like hungry wolves, called for the death of Jesus. We are told of Simon from Cyrene in Africa who was ordered to carry the cross of Jesus. It is believed that personal involvement in that cross, led to salvation for him and his family. There were women present who watched as the victims were led past them on the way to Calvary the place of execution. Others include the Centurion who supervised the crucifixion, Mary the mother of Jesus and other followers who were: 'at the foot of the Cross', and the two men who buried the body of Jesus. All these people were eyewitnesses. Their words and conversations are preserved for us in the historical Gospel accounts. Christianity however does not end with death: all four Gospel writers record the bodily resurrection of the Lord Jesus Christ from the grave on the third day after His crucifixion. Gerard uses his legal background to take us through the overwhelming evidence for the resurrection. Evidence that is direct, circumstantial and prophetic. Christianity is shown to be firmly established on the physical resurrection of its founder Jesus Christ from the dead.

Gerard describes the people and events surrounding the first Easter in imaginative and helpful detail. In each chapter he draws out insights from not only the recorded events themselves but also into the meaning and relevance of those events for us, today. Barabbas the released criminal provides a graphic illustration of every Christian: fully guilty and deserving of punishment yet amazingly saved because of Jesus who died in their place. The heavy veil in the temple at Jerusalem which was supernaturally torn signifying the end of the Jewish age and the start of a new era, marked by direct access to God through the risen Christ. Each chapter in *Were You There?* closes with a challenge to the unconverted reader to repent from their sin and personally trust in Christ. How someone becomes a Christian is spelled out. For those who are already believers the challenge is made to give our lives in full commitment to the Christ who loved us and was crucified for us but is now risen from the grave and reigns as Lord of heaven and earth. Those who have trusted Christ are challenged not only to follow Him but to make Him and His gospel known to others.

The two thieves crucified on either side of Jesus highlight the two possible responses to the gospel. We read in the Bible that both thieves initially began in unbelief and joined the reviling of Christ but later on, after hearing Jesus pray for His enemies, one thief admitted his own sins and turned to the suffering Christ for forgiveness. It is Gerard's prayer and mine that each of us reading this book would do the same.

Foreword by Jamie Southcombe, Guildford

BA, AKC, DChA, MDiv
Pastor, Grace Church Guildford

"Christ died"—that is history; "Christ died for our sins"—that is doctrine. Without these two elements, joined in an absolutely indissoluble union, there is no Christianity'. So wrote J. Gresham Machen in 1923. Almost 100 years later, Gerard Chrispin skilfully weaves these two aspects together in this excellent book, *Were You There?*. Gerard not only shows the historical reliability of Christ's death and resurrection, but he also applies the gospel truth to our lives every step of the way.

In this two-part book—primarily based on Luke 23—we meet the men and women who were there at Jesus' death (Part 1) and those who encountered the risen Lord Jesus Christ (Part 2). With biblical-fidelity and belletristic-freshness Gerard takes us through each character's experience of the death and resurrection of Jesus. The result is that even though we were not physically there at the cross or the resurrection, we are enabled to put ourselves in the shoes of those who were and learn from their responses—both good and bad—to the events of the first Easter weekend.

The book reminds us on numerous occasions that Jesus' death is, in a very real sense, for anyone. Likewise, I would commend this book to anyone. I would commend it to Christians for two reasons. First, there are helpful and thoughtful insights into the biblical text that will thrill your soul and cause your heart to be stirred afresh at the wonder that Christ could, 'love me a sinner condemned unclean'. Second, you cannot fail to read this book and not be challenged and inspired to share the gospel with those around you. I would also commend this book to you if you are not yet a Christian for one crucial reason: there is a heaven to be won and a hell to be spurned. Each one of us will stand before the judgment seat of God and your response to the truths laid out so clearly in this book will determine your eternal destiny.

An introductory word from the author

I do not shed tears easily—and maybe not often enough. But I can remember feeling so sad and sorry when I heard an amazing singer, whose relatives had suffered slavery in America, singing 'Were you there when they crucified my Lord?' As he went through the verses I felt as if I really was 'there'. Joy and triumph throbbed as he sang, 'Were you there when He rose up from the grave?' He had presented in moving song what the apostle Paul said were the two most important things to pass on to anyone. They are '*that* Christ died for our sins *according to the Scriptures, that he was buried, that* he was raised on the third day *according to the Scriptures*' (2 Corinthians 3–4).

This little book aims to bring the unique reality to you, the reader, that Jesus did indeed die for our sins and their judgment on that cruel cross, and that He conquered death in His miraculous, well attested, resurrection. We will 'meet' the individuals involved with Jesus at His crucifixion, and those who then met the risen Lord three days later. We will see what that meant to some of them, and how they were changed by the once-crucified but now risen '*Lord of glory*', the Lord Jesus Christ, our '*Immanuel*'—our '*God with us*'.

Join these individuals at the cross and after Jesus rose from the grave. If you do that, with an open and willing heart and mind, you will be blessed and maybe changed. He is still the Lord and Saviour of many today!

If you would like to go into this further, either for yourself or to arrange for others, through a related *Were You There?* Study Book, Correspondence Course or a Group Discussion Course, please contact

CPR at Christian Prison Resourcing, (CPR), PO Box 61685, London, SE9 9BL, or visit www.cprministries.org.uk

If you want to hear the chapter-by-chapter audio of this book (with the text) please go to thoughtfortheday.info and take the link for 'Were You There?'. If you are the owner of this book, you can download the entire audio recording, at no charge, by emailing info@thoughtfortheday.info Any who prefer to have a CD should ask for one from that same email address.

Before thanking the team that have produced this book, I am asked by DayOne, the publishers, to point out that the chapter on Barabbas contains conjecture that Barabbas *might have been watching* the Man, the Lord Jesus, die in his place on the cross. Whether, after release, Barabbas did that is neither affirmed nor denied in Scripture. However, the conjecture shows what *can* happen if a hardened criminal comes up against the truth of Jesus' death, and perhaps starts to realise that, as a prisoner at Pentonville exclaimed in a meeting there, 'He did it for me—I should have been there.' Barabbas went somewhere. Maybe he went to Calvary.

Thank you to a number of helpful people: to DayOne for publishing this book and especially to Mark Roberts for facilitating an early start to editing it during the Covid-19 pandemic when things were especially difficult; to Jonathan Pountney for his helpfulness and thoroughness in editing this book; to Kathryn Chedgzoy for the cover design; to Derek French of Grace Baptist Mission for recording the audio with his customary thoroughness; to Mark Alexander for his singing and music in the audio; to Georgie Knowles, a talented art student, accomplished artist, and Christian, for using part of her Covid-19 lockdown time to provide some very helpful line drawings; to my darling wife, Phillippa, for all her help, checking, and for her constructive criticisms; to my friend, David Harding for his ongoing help, comments, insights, computer ability and wisdom; to the residents at HMP Coldingley, who were my 'guinea pigs'. They received earlier versions of each successive chapter of the book under their cell doors on each Sunday morning when fear of Covid-19 had stopped chapel services. Their frank and thoughtful comments, and their kind appreciations, were extremely helpful. That first draft has been changed a lot since they received their weekly chapters! I hope it is better!

Thank you, too, to Dr Peter Williams for his kind comments, and to Jamie Southcombe and Prof Steve Taylor for their forewords. I have enjoyed working with Pete and Steve often in teams on United Beach Missions, Mission Vacances, Christian Answer and Young Life. Jamie has been a real blessing to me through his clear and concise Bible-based messages and especially the constant emphasis in his preaching of the cross and resurrection. I am privileged to have him as the pastor of the church I go to (when not in prison!). All three men are very clear thinkers, very gracious, and very well versed and respected in their respective fields of Theology, Engineering and Pastoral and Evangelistic Ministry.

Finally, may God bless you through Christ who died and rose again. May He also bless others through you.

Further introductory comments

The main Bible passages referring to the cross and resurrection are quoted in the Appendix. They follow the same order as in the Bible. Either look them up in your Bible, as with the other Bible reference given, but if you do not have access to a Bible when you read the book, you will find some basic cross and resurrection passages in the Appendix. The NIV translation is used in this book, but any good translation may be used. The references for the passages are below each chapter number and title.

Study books, correspondence courses and discussion courses

If you would like to participate in the related study books, correspondence courses or in the ciscussion courses, as an individual or as an organiser, please contact CPR at Christian Prison Resourcing, (CPR), PO Box 61685, London, SE9 9BL, or visit www.cprministries.org.uk

Read and listen on the web

Listen, free of charge and chapter-by-chapter, to the *Were You There?* audio at thoughtfortheday.info and invite others to listen. The text is written there too.

Downloads and CDs

Download the complete audio file of *Were You There?* free of charge by emailing info@thoughtfortheday.info This includes 'ISO' files to create your own audio CD.

Ready-made CDs of *Were You There?* are also available. Please ask for details by emailing info@thoughtfortheday.info

Part 1

WERE YOU THERE …
WHEN THEY CRUCIFIED MY LORD?

Pilate politicking

LUKE 23:13–25

Easter and Christmas

Long before I became a Christian, Easter was one of my favourite times of the year. School and public holidays plus Easter eggs had a lot to do with that. But it also seemed significant to me that Spring and new life came around Easter time. I came to Christ just before Easter, which then meant so much more—new life, coming out of the death and resurrection of Jesus had become personal to me. Just as I now think in one way that Christmas is a continual event to remember, so I now think that about Easter. At Christmas we remember that God became Man in the person of the Lord Jesus Christ, miraculously conceived and naturally born of a virgin. God came to live on earth as a human being! Easter tells me that Christ's death on the cross works 24/7 365 days of the year. I constantly need His forgiveness and cleansing from my sins, and the message of the cross reminds me that I can have that because Jesus' blood was shed for me. The resurrection also reminds me continually that my living Saviour, through the Holy Spirit, will never leave me nor forsake me. He is my Friend.

Eyewitnesses

Whether Easter is ahead of you or behind you as you read this, you either do know, or can come to know, Jesus as your Lord and Saviour, by putting your trust in Him and yielding your heart to Him. Jesus' death and rising again are not just for Easter for you either, but for eternity and also for each day on earth. So, let's consider Jesus' cross and empty tomb in more detail. We will seek to be eyewitnesses now as we concentrate on the cross, by examining the varied attitudes of folk who stand watching or are involved in that cruel death of 'the Son of God, who loved me and gave Himself for me' (Galatians 2:20). After all, He did all that to forgive my sins and draw me to God—and to honour and please Him by my life. Just as then, people now have different attitudes to Jesus. Some are good attitudes, and some bad—just as it is around the cross, where Jesus shed His blood took the punishment for our sin. We will look briefly, in each chapter of this book, at different people. We can learn a lot from them all. But we need to remember that there are three crosses at Calvary, and three victims. One is guilty and, as far as we know, carries on to his death in his sin. One is guilty but turns in repentance to Jesus not long before he dies. Jesus assures him of an immediate home in Heaven. Those two are cronies of Barabbas and are convicted criminals, loved by Jesus, nevertheless.[1] The One on the central cross is the Lord Jesus Christ, God the Son, bearing our sins, judgment and punishment. He will miraculously rise from the dead three days later. (We will look at that in Part 2 of this book.)

Presenting Pontius Pilate

But now we look at our first character involved in the execution of Jesus by crucifixion. He is the Roman Governor, Pontius Pilate. He is known as a hard and cruel man. He must please Caesar, his boss and Emperor in Rome, which is the occupying power in Israel. He has displeased Caesar before and is very aware that he must not do that again or this Emperor may respond, also, in a hard and cruel way. Pilate needs to control his occupied territory, Israel, and manage his relationship with the Jews, especially the ruling Council of religious leaders, or Sanhedrin, made up of the Pharisees and Sadducees and controlled by the High Priest. To cause trouble may be career-limiting and life-limiting for Pilate. But to let the Jews off too lightly may also incur Caesar's displeasure.

So, politics plays a big part in how Pilate now reacts. That means controlling the Jews without causing unnecessary upset or complaints reaching Rome. If Pilate follows what he knows, sees, hears, and logically and legally works out, he must never allow Jesus' crucifixion. But politics whispers, or even shouts, 'Put Pilate, Rome and Caesar first!' Before being too hard on this Roman Governor, we too need to be absolutely open and honest when we consider our relationship with Jesus: the word 'repent' means to admit we are wrong, tell God we are sorry, take a clear step from the wrong in our life to perform a 180-degree turn, by asking God to help us live a new life in Christ. He will indwell our hearts by the Holy Spirit, if we are real about it, and then enable and empower us to live differently. There is no room for promoting personal politics where truth and forgiveness are involved. Pilate failed. Christians must put Christ first.

Pilate's politics

So, what is it that causes Pilate to remain on the wrong side of fairness and God's forgiveness, and also the wrong side of God's eternal wrath on sin? Check Luke 23:13–25 as you read this.

- Pilate starts honestly and fairly. He seems to intend to resist the religious leaders' dishonest claim that Jesus deserves to die for inciting the people to rebel. He states that both he and King Herod have found Jesus innocent. How can he negotiate that now?
- From that seemingly fair start he strangely announces his plan to punish Jesus, the innocent one, before releasing Him. Why punish an innocent man? Maybe to give the Jews a 'result', however small compared with their demand for Jesus' blood? Pilate compromises in a relatively small way to start with. Compromises often start small—and then grow. They can give birth to a monster. Beware!
- Pilate has maintained the accepted but unjust practice of releasing someone at this time of the year, guilty or not. That is an ongoing unjust compromise. Ongoing compromises are hard to get rid of. Real repentance and faith in Christ are needed—and it still can be hard to be transparently fair and honest. We need God's help.

- The crowd shout for Jesus' blood and ask for Barabbas, a murderer, rogue, gang leader, and troublemaker to be freed instead of Jesus. Barabbas' place on the cross will now be for Jesus. Pilate now fails to insist on what he knows he should justly do. Instead, he appeals to those he should be directing. He weakly promises, again wrongly, that Jesus will be punished before His release.

- Crowd pressure builds on Pilate, with repeated cries of 'Crucify Him!' Pilate has already declared Jesus faultless. But fear of the crowd makes him act wrongly again. Their loud shouts prevail. Pilate surrenders to evil. He releases the guilty one, Barabbas, and sends the holy and sinless Son of God to die. We all should determine to go God's way and to ask God for  strength to follow Jesus closely in this evil world, which often hates His standards and always prefers its sins. Are we not like Pilate sometimes? Those who trust and follow Christ, especially in today's world, need to stay close to Him and resist peer pressure in His strength. That is why Christians read the Bible every day and spend time praying personally to God and ask for the Holy Spirit to fill and help them.

- Do you realise that, even as sin and compromise abound here (from political Pilate, to crooked religious leaders, to the cruel crowd who are so easily manipulated by those wicked leaders), God is accomplishing His perfect will at the same time? He is Sovereign. God the Father hates and condemns sin of every and any kind. Yet He formed a gracious master plan, along with Jesus. God the Father, God the Son, and God the Holy Spirit always work in perfect unison. Together they form the Triune God of Three-in-One and One-in-Three, known as the Trinity. Jesus is not only fully God from eternity to eternity: He is also the only sinless and perfect Man the world has ever seen. In loving compassion, He came from Heaven to earth where, on the cross, He paid for the sins of all sinners who will turn their back on their sins to ask Jesus to save and forgive them. So even in man's sinfulness, God lovingly and graciously plans to forgive and save each sinner who repents and believes in Jesus. Cruel and wicked men put Christ on the cross, and in so doing fulfil God the Father's eternal plan of providing a Sin-bearer and Saviour for lost men and women.

How about you?

Have you trusted the Lord Jesus Christ as your Saviour? If not, are you willing to turn your back on all your wrongdoing, resist peer pressure, and put your full confidence and trust in Jesus personally? Will you receive and believe in Him? Are you willing to follow Him as Lord of your life?

Yet to all who did receive Him, to those who believed in His name, He gave the right to become children of God. (John 1:12)

For God so loved the world that He gave His one and only Son, that whoever believes in Him shall not perish but have eternal life. (John 3:16)

NOTES

1 Mark 15:7 states that Barabbas was chained with his fellow rebels, and this is the reason for the suggestion that the two other criminals were part of the rebel group.

Barabbas bewildered

LUKE 23:17–25
ALSO REFER TO: MATTHEW 27:15–18, 20, 21; MARK 15:11; JOHN 18:39–40

They rise and needs will have
My dear Lord made away;
A murderer they save,
The Prince of life they slay.
Yet cheerful He
To suffering goes,
That He His foes
From thence might free[1]

Did Barabbas see Jesus on the cross?

We now encounter the man who had no idea that he would be crucial in the crucifixion of Jesus. Let me make it clear that I have used my imagination to build up the story where there are no hard facts to accompany the always historically correct facts which the New Testament gives. I saw an artist's impression of the people looking at Jesus as He hung on the cross, as He would have seen them. The artist included Barabbas, and that made me think.[2] The Bible does not say if Barabbas saw Jesus' crucifixion or not. If you read the Bible references provided, you will easily see where I have used the recorded facts about Barabbas simply to build up a story to illustrate one vital truth that is clearly taught. So, here we go …

Waiting for execution

… It was a hot day. Barabbas' face was covered with sweat in his cell. But that was not just because it was hot. Although he was a big, strong and rugged gang leader of some rough and tough guys, he was scared. I mean, *really* scared. He would not admit that to anyone—but it was true. His two right-hand men were waiting to be taken to their execution by crucifixion from their cells nearby.[3] But he would be the Romans' 'prize catch.' He expected to see his two gang members at those cruel Roman crosses where all their lives would end in agony. Vicious floggings would come first: many criminals had died from that alone. But, if they survived, death by crucifixion was a terrible way to go. You would be straining your lungs and heart for breath until you could breathe no longer. Nails through hands and feet were bad enough, but the thought of slow and increasingly painful suffocation terrified this hard man. Too late now, he thought, to say 'sorry' to any victims, family members, authorities, or anyone else, least of all to God Himself. All his own and his gang's crimes—the murders, cruel violent public order offences, thefts and robberies and so much else that was dirty, mean, disgusting and shabby— were too late for him to remedy now.

He remembered hearing Jesus of Nazareth preach and teach in the open air, and even healing sick people and casting out evil spirits from demon-possessed men on the hill. 'Is there hope even yet for me?' he had wondered. Jesus had told everyone, 'Repent and believe the gospel'—but he had not done that, and now it was surely too late? Many said what a change Jesus had made to and in their lives—even one of his mates had thought about it for a while, but then decided he was too bad.

His throat was dry. He waited for that four-man Roman guard team to bustle him to where he would die 'Any moment now?' Yes, he was scared—of cracking up in front of others—of feeling alone—of the huge pain to bear—and of dying. Also, since hearing from Jesus that after death there is an eternal Heaven to enjoy, or an eternal Hell to suffer, he feared what awaited him.

The dreaded moment comes—the clanking of the keys

Four sets of footsteps, paced with military precision, broke into his thoughts as they came nearer and nearer to his locked cell. He could fight, of course—but that would make things worse. He would come off worse and did not want others to see him being beaten up by the Roman soldiers. No, he would go quietly, and then try bravely to show some dignity in death. He swallowed hard. The footsteps came even closer.

Three loud bangs on the door heralded the clanking of keys in the door. A loud voice shouted, 'Barabbas! Barabbas! We've come for you now!' He swallowed again and his heart raced and throbbed. He stood up tall, shoulders back and chest out. He put a brave aggressive look on his gnarled face. He waited for the inevitable. He knew he was on his way out.

'You're free!'

'Barabbas, you're free! It's your lucky day. Come with us! Sign out and get your clobber.'

'What? Set free? Is this a cruel joke? What are you playing at?' His aggression returned to him in an instant.

'You heard what we said. Yes! Set free. Of course, if you really want to die, we will ask Pilate to choose someone else, and crucify you.'

'But why?' he exclaimed, in a daze of unbelief. *'I was guilty of so many things—and I know I did them. Is this a lousy joke? If so, I don't like it!'*

'Come on!' growled the Captain of the guard. 'Are you coming out as a free man or do we have to force you into freedom? Come on—and right now!' Two guards took an arm each, one followed behind, and the Captain led them to the gate.

Scourged then crucified

He could not believe his 'luck.' Why was he alive or free? His two gang members were not at the prison gate, so he guessed they had not been released. They would be scourged with a leather-thonged whip, embedded with bone and metal, and each man would be nailed to a cross flanking 'his' central cross. Crosses were erected at the roadside. Blood-stained, groaning, men died on them—some of them took many hours to expire. Toward the day's end, the Roman soldiers would often break the legs of victims who were still alive. The additional weight of a fully suspended body stopped any of them resisting suffocation by pushing up on their legs to help them breathe. Normally they died soon after.

A few formalities

But for now, a few formalities. A few belongings and clothes to collect. And then—suddenly it seemed—he was out! Alone! His eyes blinked unbelievingly in the bright light. He was not used to that while 'banged-up' in jail. What would he do now? Where would he go? What had really happened? Could he be sure he *really* was free? What if it was all a mistake? What if they came to get him again? And what was happening to his two gang mates?

Thinking and listening

It was rare for Barabbas to ever sit down quietly and think. But this was an unusual day. He slowly walked from the prison to the hill called Calvary. It looked like a skull: they called it 'the Place of the Skull.' Crucifixions often took place there. He sat down on a rock to try to think it through. Still bewildered, he joined the growing crowd to see if his two gang members were being crucified there. But just as he set-off he heard a conversation between two middle-aged women, who had no idea who he was.

'Yes, they have let Barabbas, of all people, go free,' she said, shaking her head sadly and disapprovingly.

   '*And you are serious, that our religious leaders whipped-up the crowd to get Pilate to crucify Jesus instead?*'

'Yes. If you had been in Jerusalem then you'd have heard loud cries of "Crucify Him!"'

   '*But He only ever did good and kind things to people. He healed the sick, made the lame walk, the blind see and the deaf hear. He cast evil spirits out of some wild men. He made some dead alive. His teaching was great—not like the boring Pharisees' fake morality. You felt the real presence of God when Jesus was around. Why on earth crucify Him?'*

'It's that stupid annual custom to free someone, however guilty. Why not free a wrongly convicted one instead? But why crucify innocent Jesus? He didn't do anything wrong to anyone.'

'So, Jesus is going to die in the place of that Barabbas, and take his punishment?'

'Yes: that's right. That is the real crime—and allowed by Pilate. It's wrong and unfair.'

Conscience strikes—the three crosses

Barabbas was glad that they did not recognise him. He merged into the crowd going to the Place of the Skull. He felt a double-deep pang of conscience when he saw together the three crosses. He felt guilty, in his now quieter frame of mind, when he saw his two accomplices. Nailed, blood-stained, and in obvious pain they joined in the cruel crowd's insults and blasphemies directed at the man nailed to the central cross, Jesus. A crown of long thorns, crammed into His brow, spread even more blood on his battered face. In different languages a sign said, 'The King of the Jews.'

Barabbas heard Jesus respond with moving words: 'Father forgive them, for they don't know what they do' (Luke 23:34). Suddenly one of them stopped swearing and shouting and said something quieter to Jesus that Barabbas did not quite hear. Jesus replied with a smile on His battered face. The man looked instantly at peace.

Much else strangely miraculous was going on around those crosses, including the frightening onset of darkness. Was light dawning for Barabbas as enveloping darkness at mid-day blotted out the sun like a huge eclipse? Barabbas had seen and heard enough. He was broken. He felt the blame for getting his friends into trouble and now execution. They were dying. But he was even more worried that a completely innocent, loving, and righteous Man—who many said was God in the flesh—should die in *his* place, for *his* wrongdoing, and take *his* punishment in that broken body. Yes, he left Calvary a broken man—sad and aware of his wickedness and selfishness, and ashamed yet strangely grateful that Jesus had died in his place for him.

A picture of us all

The name 'Barabbas' means 'son of the father.' This sinful man pictures every man and woman alive. We are all the son or daughter of our father. Like him we have all sinned against God and hurt others. Whether our sins are obvious to all or not, God says, 'All *have sinned and fall short of the glory of God*' (Romans 3:23), and '*there is* none *righteous, no* not one!' (Romans 3:10). Each one of us has offended a holy and righteous God and ignored or broken His commandments. Most of us would have to admit that in different ways we have hurt others too. We have lived selfishly. We too deserve judgment and punishment for our sins. The Bible says that after death we must 'face judgment' (Hebrews 9:27), and Jesus spoke about the broad way that leads to that judgment, and the narrow way that leads to eternal life (Matthew 7:13–14). We *all* need to turn from our sins, say (and mean) we are sorry to God, and ask Him to forgive us because the Lord Jesus Christ bore all our sins and their punishment on that cruel cross for each of us (1 Peter 2:24; Isaiah 53:5–6). But until we turn, trust and receive Jesus in our hearts, as our risen Lord and Saviour, we are lost forever (Luke 13:3, 5). But the 'good news' is that, if you do confess and forsake your sins and ask Jesus to enter your life, He *will* save you. Have you done that? Why not do it now?

'it was me who should have been there'

I remember asking the guys at a Bible study at Pentonville Prison in

London what they would have felt like *if* they had been Barabbas and *if* he had seen Jesus being crucified. One prisoner said, very seriously, 'I would say that it was me who should have been there. He died in my place—and it's not fair.' He hit the nail on the head—and everyone who trusts in Jesus and His death on the cross can say that. But remember that 'God so loved the world that He gave His one and only Son, that whoever believes in Him shall not perish but have eternal life' (John 3:16). Thank God too, for 'the Son of God, who loved me and gave Himself for me' (Galatians 2:20). Trust in Him!

NOTES

1 From 'My song is love unknown' by John Ireland and Samuel Crossman circa 1664.

2 It is rare for me to adopt this approach, but no Bible truth is compromised by it, of course.

3 This is a supposition based on Mark 15:7.

Murderous mob

LUKE 23:13–25 (NIV)

The tyranny of peer pressure

Now we tackle something most of us experience at some time and hate: the power and wicked effect of peer pressure. We will see it at work on a large scale now, when a murderous mob corrupts even occupying Rome's powerful justice system. As we have seen, Pontius Pilate, Roman Governor and judge, wrongly and unjustly gives in to the crowd, who are so easily manipulated by the corrupt religious leaders. Pilate knows that Jesus is innocent of their fake charges. But now Jesus must die.

Fickle crowds

Only a short time earlier, the crowds went wild to welcome Jesus on Palm Sunday, as he rode into Jerusalem on a donkey. They knew He was the Saviour, but they guessed the wrong *kind* of saviour. They hoped he would lead them to rebel against the Roman occupation of Israel. So, as Jesus went to town, in Jerusalem, on a donkey—which is how a king ceremonially entered a city—they 'went to town' in another way. They raved and repeatedly shouted 'Hosanna' (meaning 'save now') and threw their clothes and palm branches in the road for Him to pass over as He rode the donkey along (Matthew 21:9, 15; John 12:13). They had seen Jesus' love for those He healed, comforted, and helped. He had even raised some dead people to life. But those people who were in the earlier crowds, now shouting for His blood, obviously did not understand or heed what He was teaching.

Asking too much?

Jesus wanted them to turn from their wrongs, both nationally and personally, and put their trust in Him as Lord. Each of them needed to trust and follow

Him. They also needed to believe and obey God's written word, namely the Scripture. That was asking too much of many people, and the 'Jesus craze' passed. Others, however, like His disciples, experienced a real about-turn in their lives causing them also to trust and follow Jesus and His word. Many Jews were sick of the shallow and sham living of so many of their religious leaders, especially the Pharisees. They 'talked the talk' but did not 'walk the walk', or even attempt to walk it. The Bible calls that 'hypocrisy'. It means 'play acting'. Jesus unreservedly condemned it, even more than many obvious and easily recognised sins (Matthew 23:23–29). So, those crooked religious leaders hated Jesus, and schemed to kill Him, with the ever-cynical support and help from their sly High Priest (John 5:18; 18:13).

Religious sinners need to be saved too—even leaders

That is why their religious leaders wickedly manipulated the once admiring crowd against Jesus and insisted on His death. We will examine those leaders later in this book, but, for now, please note that a man or woman can be extremely religious and still not know or please God. That is true if that person is nominally 'Christian' or from any other religion. He or she is nevertheless a sinner needing to be saved from sin, self, judgment and Hell (Hebrews 9:27). That does not happen just by being religious.

What the good news is

The message of the Christian gospel (which means 'good news') starts with the unpleasant fact that I have offended God's righteous and holy laws and so deserve His punishment. It also stresses that I am not and never can be good enough for Heaven through what I am or what I can do (Romans 3:23). But the good news is that the Lord Jesus Christ can and wants to save me (1 Timothy 1:15). He wants to change my life now and give me eternal life. As He changes me to serve Him, God will give me His peace and joy (Romans 15:13). The risen and living Lord guarantees that as soon as I come to trust Him, He will instantly give me eternal life. He also gives it to all who ask Him into their lives and enters their lives by the Holy Spirit (John 14:27).

Back to the fickle crowd

Now let us get back to the fickle and murderous mob. Even when Judge Pilate says he has examined the case against Jesus and dismissed it as wrong and unjust, they are manipulated to bellow out with one voice, *'Crucify Him! Crucify Him!'* (Luke 23:21). Pilate tries to talk them out of that terrible and biased prejudice at least twice more. But a violent mob, full of hatred, has no time for justice, truth or fairness. (Mind you, most of them would hope for and expect it for themselves from others!) Pilate tells them he and King Herod reached the same conclusion after hearing and considering the facts. That makes no difference to the mob.

When, finally, Pilate says he will punish innocent Jesus before them (you might ask, 'Why?') and then let Him go, they again cry out for His blood. This usually fearsome and strong Roman leader crumbles. He releases the notorious murderer, insurrectionist, thief, and gang leader, Barabbas. His name, Bar-abbas, literally means 'the son of the father'. As such he is a picture of us all—we all are sons or daughters of our fathers. Just as our fathers committed sins and need Jesus' forgiveness, so do we.

Jesus loved them, died and rose again

But Jesus loved them, died and rose again for them, and offered to change them from within. Similarly, today, He loves you and wants to bless you, too. For centuries men and women have received Him as their living Lord and Saviour. You need to do the same. Repent with your whole heart and trust Him also wholeheartedly because He is still the only Saviour (Acts 4:12; John 14:6). He will save you from sin in three ways. He will forgive your past to save you from punishment. He will also save, bless, strengthen, help and change you now on earth by His Holy Spirit as He gives you eternal life. He will save you and receive you in Heaven when you die.

What we can learn from the murderous mob

The murderous mob teaches us two important lessons for life:

First, never follow a crowd because it 'shouts loudly.' The well-travelled 'broad way' leading to Hell is broad enough for all kinds of beliefs, errors and sins. Few on it accept Jesus' invitation to move off it onto the 'narrow way' to life and Heaven. But God gives strength, peace and joy to those who repent and make that choice, by His grace (Matthew 7:13–14).

Second, never trust teaching about God unless you can find it endorsed in His word, the Bible. Others will have their views, but remember that no religion, religious belief, procedure, ceremony, good works or person other than Jesus can ever save you.

Only trusting in Jesus can do that! Trust in Him, now! (2 Corinthians 6:2).

Simon selected

LUKE 23:24–27 (NIV)
ALSO REFER TO: MATTHEW 27:32; MARK 15:21

Who is Simon, and where is Cyrene?

So far, in Luke chapter 23, we have met Pontius Pilate, Barabbas, and that fickle mob that cruelly yelled for Jesus to die. Now please meet Simon of Cyrene. Cyrene is an old North African port with a strong Greek influence in what we now call Libya. It is a long-established Jewish settlement and the oldest and most important of Greek cities in the region. It was bequeathed to Rome in 96 BC and became a Province in 74 BC. Acts 6:9 tells us that Jewish settlers from Cyrene were in Jerusalem and saw the Holy Spirit fall on the church on that amazing Day of Pentecost.

Simon is mentioned both in Matthew 27:32 and in Mark 15:21. He is the father of Alexander and Rufus. Rufus and his mother *may be* the Christians mentioned in Romans 16:13. She was later well known to the Apostle Paul.

Did Simon's first close contact with Jesus lead to family conversions?

Perhaps Simon's family had their first contact with Jesus and His gospel through the sad event that we now are about to examine. If so, it just shows how such an unpromising start can be used by God to bring great blessing to people. *Maybe* Simon, Rufus, or his mother (or possibly Alexander) all came to faith in Christ, and received the assurance of eternal life, through Simon first seeing Jesus carrying His cross, and then being forced to do what we examine in this chapter.

In the closing greetings Paul sends to the Christians in Rome, he says, 'Greet Rufus, chosen in the Lord, and his mother, who has been a mother to me, too' (Romans 16:13). We have no supporting evidence one way or the other whether the Rufus mentioned there is the same Rufus as Simon of Cyrene's son. He could well have been. Of course, Simon could have become a Christian independently anyway, whether his family members received Christ or not through or because of him. We just do not know.

But perhaps these events did start the process that God used to bring Simon to repent personally of his sins and ask Jesus Christ to forgive him, cleanse him, and come to live in his heart, to bless and to lead him as his Lord. But we cannot say for sure if that happened or not.

The 'root out of dry ground'

Although we cannot be dogmatic about their conversions being started through God using these sad events, that strong possibility is an encouraging reminder that God can save anyone, anywhere, at any time. Our God can always do the 'impossible'—so He certainly could do this! If so, this might be called *'a root out of dry ground'* that produces amazing fruitfulness, but in a far lesser way than the Bible describes Jesus by using that phrase in Isaiah 53:2.

Humanly speaking, Jesus was wrongly 'suspected of' having been born illegitimately. While always being sinless and perfect, and the Lord of Glory in human flesh, Jesus had very humble human origins. The average onlooker would say that there was very little 'going for' the carpenter's son. He later would die as a crucified criminal, after bitter betrayal, desertion by disciples, cruel rejection, fake justice and merciless flogging. All that did not suggest the floods of amazing eternal blessing and joy yet to come. Yet that 'root out of dry ground' produced overwhelming and abundant fruitfulness in the worldwide blessing for the millions who have trusted Him as Saviour. Did what must have then seemed to Simon the worst day of his life result finally in his family and himself being saved, and maybe others through them? In God's amazing grace that is quite possible. If you are finding things going very wrong for you right now, take heart!

Meanwhile, please remember that, just like Simon of Cyrene, we are all guilty sinners, and have sins that need to be forgiven by God if we are to receive eternal life and so end our days in Heaven.

What Simon was made to do

Remember that Judge Pilate unjustly decided to condemn Jesus to death, although he was personally convinced of His innocence—as was King Herod—and had said so. Jesus had been blindfolded and punched in the face by rough Roman soldiers who 'played a game' with him. He was also severely physically weakened by a vicious and cruel Roman flogging, which killed off many crucifixion victims before they could even get to their cross. A crown of long nail-like thorns is put on His battered head (Matthew 27:29). Now, He is so badly bruised, and wounded with a lacerated back, that Isaiah 52:14 prophetically predicts, *'His appearance was so disfigured beyond that of any man and His form marred beyond human likeness.'* The second part of Isaiah 53:2 adds, *'He had no beauty or majesty to attract us to Him, nothing in his appearance that we should desire Him.'* Jesus is now led off to be executed by crucifixion and he is now so weakened by the cruel assaults on Him that he cannot carry the heavy and crude cross Himself. The soldiers seize unsuspecting Simon, and put

Jesus' cross on this North African, as he follows behind the battered and bleeding Saviour. They make him carry that cross for Jesus. Many people follow them. (We will look next time at the women who were there, called the 'Daughters of Jerusalem.')

But what if Simon did not turn to Jesus?

We have seen that it is well possible that Simon did turn to Jesus and that God used that to influence family members to trust in Christ too. But it is equally valid to assume that Simon did not turn to Jesus. Just for argument's sake, and to make another point to learn from, we now ask and answer the question, 'But what if Simon did *not* turn to Jesus personally as his Saviour and so was *not* "born again?"' What lessons do we learn from that assumption that Simon carried the cross for Jesus to Calvary but did not become a Christian?

No other way

The first thing to say is obvious but necessary. If Simon never turned from his sins and asked for God's forgiveness by putting all His trust in Jesus, he is not in Heaven today, but in Hell. He did not and could not merit forgiveness by anything he did, including carrying the cross for our wounded and physically weakened Saviour (Ephesians 2:8–9).

The second matter to note is that Simon of Cyrene's name never appears again in the pages of Scripture. Not once! We are not told in the Bible whether he trusted in Jesus or not. There is nothing specific to say he did. We may need to remind ourselves, and others, that we do not become Christians by doing what someone else tells us to do, good as it may be. If we take up our own cross, it means *we* have repented from *our* sins, put all *our* trust in Jesus, and decided by God's grace to follow Him wholeheartedly. And we can only do that as individuals. Mark 8:34 says that Jesus *'called the crowd to him al*ong with his disciples and said: *"If anyone would come after me, he must deny himself and take up his cross and* *follow me.'"* In Luke 14:27 Jesus adds, *"anyone who does not carry his cross and follow me cannot be my disciple."* Real repentance includes the attitude of saying 'No' to ourselves and saying 'Yes' to Jesus: each of us has to decide to make Jesus our Lord and take up our own cross.

What follows when I take up my cross?

It follows that if I really repent from my sins that also involves me putting King Jesus on the throne of my life to run it His way. Taking up the cross is what a man literally did when he went to his own crucifixion—just as Jesus did, albeit helped by Simon. In short it means that at the same time as I ask Jesus into my life as my Saviour from sin, judgment and Hell, I put myself 100% under His holy but loving Lordship and control (Romans 14:9). I make a decision in principle to die to my own choices, and I ask Jesus to be my living Lord, dwelling in me by the Holy Spirit, to lead my life the way He wants it to go. That is why the Bible, God's written word, becomes my final authority and my life map. It is why I read it and pray every day to my loving Master and Saviour. It is also why I ask the Holy Spirit to keep on filling me so I can keep on following Christ (Ephesians 5:18). I now seek to be dead to self and sin and alive to Jesus, God's will, and God's word, through the Holy Spirit. This is an ongoing work of God's grace. I cannot 'work it up' myself. Remember that we have just seen that Jesus said that unless I take up my cross every day like that I *'cannot* be [His] disciple'.

Another cross

I repeat that no-one can make me bear my cross or do it for me. It is *my* cross, and *I* alone can *deny myself* to take it up for Him. But there is another cross for us to consider even more closely and openly. It is the cross that Jesus was nailed to in my place, for my sins, to take the just and holy punishment of God the Father against me for the sins I have committed against Him. There is nothing magic or holy about the wood of the cross itself, of course. It is rather that it was there that Jesus died and so can enable every sinner who has repented, believed and started following Him, to now praise and proclaim with both shame and gratitude, *'the Son of God, who loved me and gave himself for me'* (Galatians 2:20). No-one can be saved now or in eternity until he or she realises that on that cross everything that could be done to save him or her was 'finished' (meaning 'accomplished') by the Lord Jesus Christ (John 19:30).

If you do not come to Jesus like that, through His cross in order to take up yours, you too, like Simon, may not be heard of again as someone who knows and follows Jesus. If you do deny yourself and trust wholly in Jesus, many others will both hear and see that now you are under the 'new management' of the Lord Jesus Christ, the once crucified and now living Saviour and Lord of all who repent and trust Him. You will witness to others what Jesus has done for you.

The wisest choice

The wisest choice anyone ever can make is to repent, trust in Jesus personally, and ask Him for His help to follow, live for, and witness about Him as Lord. Are *you* that person?

Women weeping

LUKE 23:23–27; 47–49; 55–56 (NIV)

The 'man' for the job

A missionary society, then named the 'Worldwide Evangelisation Crusade' (WEC for short) had an unofficial motto that 'A woman is the "man" for the job.' The Bible teaches that men are normally responsible to lead in Christian work, but there are so many examples where God uses women in all sorts of situations and challenges, either on their own or with their husbands, quite apart from the unique role that a good mum or grandma has in the family. Women often put men to shame for their willingness to sacrifice in Christian work.

Women at the cross

We now look at the women present as Jesus is about to be crucified upon Calvary's cross. As we look at three different, but closely related, situations covered in Luke chapter 23, we meet first some women from Jerusalem. We will then twice meet some of the women who followed Jesus to Calvary from His native Galilee. As the crow flies, Jerusalem is about 60 miles from the nearest part of Galilee. Let us learn from both sets of women, as we look at the three 'snapshots.' The Jerusalem group was probably mixed—almost certainly some loved Jesus, but some did not. The Galilean women had probably walked at least 60 miles to show their love and reverence for Him. In His death, as in His life and teaching, Jesus divides people into two groups: those who trust Him and His word, and follow Him; and those who do not, however they express and live out that unbelief or disobedience.

What can we learn from those women from Jerusalem and those from Galilee about what it really means to trust, love and follow Jesus?

Snapshot 1—Luke 23:27–31

Our first snapshot of women at the cross is from verses 27–31. We take up where we left off when Simon of Cyrene was made to carry the cross of Jesus behind the wrongly condemned Son of God. After His cruel humiliation and beating by the soldiers (Luke 22:64), and scourging (John 19:1), Jesus was bruised and bleeding. These 'Daughters of Jerusalem' in the large crowd follow Jesus and Simon to the hill called 'Calvary.' Jesus will soon be crucified there, nailed to His cross.

Dying for us

We now can look back at history and see Him dying for us, bearing our judgment and punishment in our place (1 Peter 2:24). We can now be forgiven if we turn from our sins and trust Jesus personally. Some at Calvary will recognise the unfair crucifixion of this guiltless victim of 'rough justice,' and bigoted, religious but Godless, leaders who manipulated and spurred the crowd on to be a cruel mob. Many of those in the crowd earlier howled for Jesus' blood like a pack of vicious wolves.

For or against Jesus?

We do not know who amongst those women is *for* Jesus and who is *against* Him. Mourners often gave loud theatrical 'performances' in those days. Some of them openly 'mourned and wailed' for the dead person without any feeling for them at all. It was a paid job for some and a hobby for others. But some would be sincerely heart-broken at the loss of the dead person. It is easy to believe that many people who had been personally blessed by Jesus, and their grateful relatives, now sincerely mourn His loss, even though those of them who have put their trust in Him know they will see Him again in Heaven after they die. Some who have not yet trusted and followed Jesus personally will nevertheless appreciate the wisdom and good common sense of what He taught and the loving care He showed, without having turned to Him personally. We do not know how each of these Jerusalem women felt. Some may have been friendly and sincere, others may have been hostile and insincere, but hopefully some loved and followed the Lord Jesus Christ, or were on the way to doing so.

Jesus too preoccupied and stressed?

You might think that as Jesus passes by these women on His way to die on the cross, in the hardest and darkest hours of His earthly life as a human being, that He is so preoccupied and stressed with His own horrific situation that he has nothing to say to them. He could justifiably avoid making any helpful comments to them that show His unfailing concern for them. In fact, it is a token of His immense and divinely perfect love for others that He even notices them.

But He turns to them and calls them 'Daughters of Jerusalem.' He then says 'do not weep for Me.' How unselfish and courageous is that? But He goes further and tells them to weep for themselves and their children. He says that childless women will one day be regarded as more 'blessed' than those with children.

Why does Jesus warn them?

Why does Jesus warn them? Perhaps, apart from any future problems and troubles yet to be faced in troubled Jerusalem, He knows that unless each one of these mainly *insincere* women *sincerely* repents from their sins and believes in Him, they will be eternally lost (John 3:36). He also knows that those who are on the way towards trusting Him can get side-tracked or put off when they will learn how opposed many are towards Him and His followers. Jesus knows that cruel persecution will hit the early church after His departure (Acts 8:1). But, even at this stage as He goes to die on the cross, He prepares people to repent and trust Him by warning them. It is out of love for them that He warns them: He wants to see them in

Heaven after they die. What amazing love, compassion and selflessness we see now in Jesus, our 'Emmanuel' (or 'God with us').

Second snapshot—Luke 23:47–49

Verses 47–49 give the second snapshot. It is of the second group of women who so love and trust the Lord Jesus that they have walked all that way from Galilee to be near Him. They do not stand in the main crowd—this is not a 'performance' for them to watch or enjoy, but the deathbed of

One they love, trust and follow. From the crowd's edge, these godly, caring women witness three hours darkness descend at mid-day on the cross and blot out the sun, as the great Creator-Saviour commits Himself to His Father in Heaven and dies, bearing their sins and suffering their judgment. In the temple, the thick coloured curtain or veil keeping the Temple's Most Holy Place inaccessible to humanity, is torn in two from top to bottom, thereby signifying that, through the death of Jesus, the way to God is now open for all to enter into a relationship with God, if they will turn from sin and trust in Him (Luke 23:44–46).

These women will rejoice to hear

These women will rejoice to hear the Roman centurion praise God and declare two vital truths: *'Surely this was a righteous Man'* and, *'Surely this Man was the Son of God'* (Luke 23:47; Mark 15:39). They will also rejoice to see the once bloodthirsty, rough and crude spectators in the crowd now beat their breasts and leave. Do some repent and trust Christ? Will some do so later? Maybe some do or will. But mere sorrow is not the same as repentance: it is sorrow that causes a sinner to *turn from sin*. Perhaps some are among those who later respond to God when Peter will preach the gospel on the Day of Pentecost and 3,000 will be saved (Acts 2:37–41). Never underestimate the value of circumstances and events that God uses to prepare people to see the guilt of their wrong actions and attitudes and make an about-turn from sin to embrace Jesus as their Lord and Saviour. Sometimes a sinner receives Christ as soon as he hears the good news about Jesus. Sometimes it is days, weeks, months or years later that he is converted. Very sadly, sometimes he enters Hell knowing he should have repented and believed in Jesus: that is both sad and tragic. Be warned!

Third snapshot—Luke 23:55–57

In verses 55–57, we see a few of these same women follow a rich tomb owner, and rare-believing Council member, Joseph of Arimathea. Pilate lets him collect and place Jesus' body in his own new tomb (Matthew 27:60). These women are Mary Magdalene and Mary, the mother of James and Joses, and probably some others from their group. They both see the tomb and Jesus' body in it. They plan to go home to prepare spices for embalming the body in that tomb. So, they know Jesus is dead and where He was laid. Later, they will also be some of the key witnesses of Jesus' resurrection from the dead. Later still, they will meet the risen Jesus personally! These women are truly committed to the Lord: they rest on the Sabbath because they obey the commandments. Those who love Jesus do keep His commands (John 14:15; 15:10). Still today the fourth commandment bids us keep His day holy for Him each week, as far as we can (Exodus 20:8–11). This we do on the Lord's day, the first day of each week, which is the Christian Sabbath and the day we also remember Jesus' resurrection from the dead.

Be encouraged!

Be encouraged! God loves, saves, blesses and uses seemingly 'ordinary' people. Yes, He still saves 'ordinary' folks now. He still uses them as His important witnesses today, to share with others how they came to know Him and the great difference He has made, is making, and will make eternally.

How about you?

He loves you, knows about you, and can save and bless you too. You may not believe it right now, but if you trust and surrender to Him, He will not only forgive you and give you eternal life: He will grow you in your Christian life, and use you in the future to glorify Him, encourage other Christians, and help others to trust Him as their Saviour too. Be sure to trust in this crucified and risen Saviour.

Criminal converted

LUKE 23:32–44 (NIV)
ALSO REFER TO: MATTHEW 27:38, 44; MARK 15:27, 32; JOHN 19:18

Two hard 'lifers'

We have 'met' a number of people who, for different reasons, meet or are near the Lord Jesus Christ as he is about to be crucified in the centre of three crosses at Calvary's hill called the 'Place of the Skull.' The people we now 'meet' there still seem to interest people keenly today, whether inside or outside prison. Why? Two hard 'lifers' are dying on crosses. Jesus is dying between them. We will see the equivalent of a deathbed conversion for one prisoner. How about the other prisoner? He seems very hard-hearted as his life ebbs away. His opportunity to make sure he goes to Heaven after he dies, by repenting and believing in Christ, is passing away fast. Whether he realises it or not, Hell awaits him if he does not turn from sin and trust Jesus Christ.

Take that urgent opportunity

Make sure that *you* take that urgent opportunity to receive Christ. Jesus died on the cross for you, to bear all your sin and take its punishment for you. Sinless Jesus had no sin of His own to pay for. At Calvary, He sacrifices Himself for sinners like you and me. He dies as the pure and innocent sacrifice to suffer God's eternal wrath which we all deserve for our sins against God and others. Only those who repent and trust wholly in Him are forgiven and saved: those who do not, remain unforgiven and will be subject to that wrath (John 3:16, 36).

Jesus flanked by members of Barabbas' gang[1]

We met Barabbas earlier in this book. This notoriously cruel, hard, and dishonest man was guilty of murder, robbery, theft, and promoting serious and violent public order offences. He escaped dying on the centre cross when the ungodly religious leaders manipulated the mob to pressurise Pilate, Israel's Roman Governor, to release Barabbas and crucify Jesus instead. So, Jesus now must die on that centre cross, flanked by the two condemned members of Barabbas' gang. They, and Jesus, face a cruel, painful, and often lingering death. Jesus is innocent. They are guilty. They provide the watching crowd with free and sick 'entertainment.'

'Father forgive them': forgive who?

The two guilty men now hear Jesus pray, *'Father, forgive them, for they do not know what they are doing.'* Who is He praying for? His executioners, the Romans? Or the ignorant and lost crowd? Or perhaps the crooked religious leaders who spur the crowd on in their hatred? There is another possible answer. Jesus may be referring to these two condemned prisoners. Christ loves prisoners. He saves many. He wants to save people like them. But, even more, He wants to save people who are 'prisoners' of their own sins. Their guilty consciences are imprisoned in their sinful hearts unless, and until, Jesus sets them free. Christ looks forward to sharing Heaven with them. So, no doubt, Jesus has in mind, also, that *all* those around His cross need God's forgiveness—and so does anyone today who has never come to Christ.

Insults

The two criminals hear the religious leaders' shout their insulting sneer at Jesus, *'He saved others; let Him save Himself if He is the Christ of God, the Chosen One.'* The soldiers steal their punchline and throw the same kind of jibe at Jesus. This time they make fun of the notice Pilate put on Christ's cross, *'THIS IS THE KING OF THE JEWS.'*

Now the criminals also get involved in insulting Jesus. Mark's account adds that they both insult Him. But then something unexpected happens. God is at work in the heart of one of Barabbas' condemned cronies. Has the 'penny dropped' now for him? Is the Holy Spirit showing this dying man who Jesus is, and what He is doing? Maybe God shows him Jesus' love and compassion by the way the Son of God responds in love and grace in the face of such unwarranted cruelty?

'Don't you fear God?'

Now he speaks to his fellow gang member on the third cross who hurls *'insults'* at Christ. He asks, *'Don't you fear God?'* He reminds him that they both are receiving the same deserved death sentence. (It seems their offences could well have been similar to what Barabbas had done.) He then realises that he is sinful, but Jesus is sinless and perfect. He volunteers, *'We are pu*nished justly, for we are getting what our deeds deserve. But this Man has done nothing wrong.'

The Holy Spirit is working within him

When someone comes to Christ for forgiveness, God shows them that they are a guilty sinner needing mercy and forgiveness. This dying criminal has now seen for himself that this is true. The Holy Spirit is working within him. Do *you* see *your* need to confess your sins to Jesus and ask Him to forgive you and take over in your life? That is all so important. It does not just 'happen.'

'Jesus remember me'

But then he prays a vital prayer for himself. He wants to turn from his sin and ask Jesus to become his Saviour and Lord. He prays to the Lord Jesus Christ this crucial and simple prayer from his heart: *'Jesus remember me when You come in Your kingdom.'*

That is his prayer. It is heartfelt, direct and humble. Does he expect an encouraging reply from Jesus? He is neither religious, nor a good-living person. But he is a guilty sinner who asks the Friend and Saviour of sinners to save him. That is why Jesus is on that cross: to pay the price of His own blood to save anyone who would ask Him humbly to do so. Remember too: Jesus died in *your* place and bore *your* sins and *your* punishment, so He can offer *you* forgiveness and eternal life.

Jesus' immediate response—to him and to you!

Jesus responds to him immediately and clearly: *'I tell you the truth,'* [He always does!] *'today you will be with Me in Paradise.'*

This is Jesus' instant answer to a 'bad' sinner's sincere and heartfelt prayer. Your sins may or may not be like his: but you, like us all, have committed many sins of your own. If *you* turn to the Lord like this convict did, the Lord Jesus Christ becomes *your* Saviour *immediately*. A new life of living for Him, learning from Him and His word, the Bible, and enjoying having fellowship with, and meeting with, your new Christian family and friends begins! There are many dangers, temptations and problems too—but Jesus is always with you to help and guide you, right from the start.

Is Jesus your Saviour yet? If not, why not ask Him? He is only a prayer away. Come to Him now, if you have not yet done so. John 1:12 says, *'to all who received Him, [the Lord Jesus Christ] to those who believed in His name, He gave the right to become children of God.'*

NOTES

1 Mark 15:7 says Barabbas was jailed with his gang members, and the assumption here is that he escaped the penalty, and they didn't.

Religious rulers ridicule

LUKE 23:13–25, 35 (NIV)

Deliberate manipulation

Now we will focus on the sad fact that the leading 'Religious rulers' oppose and ridicule the Lord Jesus Christ in His hour of need. In Jesus' day, local rulers were always religious people. The ruling Council (Sanhedrin) comprised of Sadducees, Pharisees, priests, high priests and family members, scribes, and elders. It was this group of people who deliberately turned the crowd into a mob against Jesus. They illustrate the fact that looking 'religious' (of any religion) does not necessarily mean that you know the God of truth, love, care and holiness. Religion saves no-one: only the Lord Jesus Christ saves, and only if there is sorrow for sin, turning from it, and a personal trust in Him.

Why the religious men influence the mob

You can see why the religious men influence the mob. The Roman Governor, Pontius Pilate, first questioned Jesus and then sent Him to be heard before King Herod. By the time that Jesus arrives at Herod's palace the chief priests and law teachers are already before the King. They are 'vehemently accusing' Jesus (Luke 23:10).

Pilate then includes the 'people' with the rulers and chief priests, in his follow-up questions to Jesus. He decides, after that, to punish Him and release Him. He tells his hearers so. He argues that he finds the charges are unjustified, and neither can King Herod find Jesus guilty of anything deserving death. They are both very well-known and experienced judges! The crooked team of prosecutors and the 'people' they influence now cry *'with one voice'* but with two goals: *'Away with this man!'* and *'Release*

Barabbas to us!' When a crowd like that is with them, behaving as a blood-thirsty mob, their voice becomes even louder.

Pilate makes an appeal instead of announcing a verdict

Yet Pilate then amazingly *appeals 'to them again.'* Given that this 'hard' Governor of mighty occupying Rome, schooled in the famed Roman Law, decides to release Jesus on evidence independently heard and evaluated by two experienced judges, does he *really* need to *appeal 'to them again?'* Why does he not simply tell them his verdict and go ahead, as is normal? And what is their response to his appeal? They keep shouting 'Crucify Him! Crucify Him!' Does he call the famed Roman Guard onto the scene to enforce his verdict and orders? No! *'For the third time'* he tries to reason with unreasonable haters of Jesus—the rulers, the religious, and the people who are the manipulated 'engine room' of trouble. Pilate asks what Jesus' crime is and restates there are no grounds to find Him guilty of death or deserving 'the death penalty.' He repeats his considered and already announced judgment, *'Therefore I will have Him punished and release Him.'* Surely that must be the end of this Hearing?

Pilate gives in

But no! See what frightening power a manipulated crowd that shouts loudly can exert. 'But with those loud shouts they insistently demand that [Jesus] be crucified,' says verse 23. The rebel high priests, religious rulers, and people out of Pilate's lawful control, win the day. Pilate gives in! Their shouts prevail. Pilate grants their demand. He releases the murderer, robber, thief, violent troublemaker and gang leader, Barabbas. Why? Because the religiously led mob insistently asked for that loudly! Who would have believed that possible? And Pilate surrenders *'Jesus to their will.'* Mob rule wins—empowered by religious hypocrisy and dishonest leadership. That is an evil combination. The rulers will mark their triumph with lying sneers at Jesus on the cross: *'He saved others; let Him save Himself if He is the Christ of God, the Chosen One.'*

What can we learn?

What can we all learn from these amazing and extremely sad happenings? How can these things possibly help *me* today in my own life, and teach me something important about how I should live? Everything in God's  word, the Bible, is there for a purpose. Sometimes it can be hard to grasp what that is. However, if we ask God to help us to learn and understand as we read His word, the same Holy Spirit who inspired the Bible to be written as God's perfect and infallible word, can cause it to be unmistakably understood and followed by willing hearers. Every person who puts all their trust in the death of Jesus on the cross as the penalty paid for all the sins they have committed and receives Christ in their heart as their living Saviour, will find that God speaks personally to them through the Bible, His word. So, let us now consider some observations about these 'Religious Rulers,' and draw some lessons from them.

First, no religion can save

First, again note that *no-one* can be accepted by God just by being 'religious.' Whether that is a genuine Christian religion, a nominal one, or not a Christian one at all, no-one can be forgiven by God or come to know Him by being religious, however sincere that person may be.

Second, neither can good works save anyone

Second, doing good, worthy as it may seem—and far better than doing bad—cannot save you either. You can only be *saved* because Jesus, the *Saviour*, took your sin and paid for it with His blood as if it was His own sin, and rose again in triumph over sin and death. At the same time that you trust in Him, He puts His sinless and perfect righteousness into your bankrupt moral account and counts all His spotless righteousness as yours. He was punished for your sins. You are saved by His death, resurrection and righteousness. Good deeds cannot and do not save, only Jesus Christ does. He does that when you turn from wrong and put all your trust in Him.

Ephesians 2:8–9 is rightly often quoted. It says, *'For it is by grace you have been saved, through faith—and this not from yourselves, it is the gift of God—not by works, so that no-one can boast.'*

Third, have the courage to do what is right

Third, ask God to give you the courage always to do what you know is right. If you are not sure, check it in the Bible or with keen reliable Christian friends or leaders. Never do anything through the power of peer pressure, or through the fear of those who shout loudly, or because you are in a minority. Be true to Jesus no matter who, what, where or when. He will strengthen you if you develop your relationship with Him (Isaiah 40:31).

Fourth, pray for those who oppose you

Fourth, pray for those who oppose you unfairly, for those who might not like you and may even hate you, and for those who *seem* too bad to change.

Think about arch-persecutor Saul, who became the Apostle Paul. He was a sincere, but sincerely wrong, religious ruler responsible for the deaths and devastation of many Christians and churches. Who could possibly expect that he would be saved by yielding to Jesus and become the most famous Christian missionary, evangelist, and church maker the world has ever seen? Not only his name, but his whole life was changed. Through Paul (no longer 'Saul') so much of the New Testament was penned. When first converted, the early Christians dare not believe he was converted, in case it was a trick to persecute them! But God worked in his heart and used ordinary 'scared' Christians to lead him to, and deepen his faith in, Jesus!

Remember that Jesus said, in the famous Beatitudes He taught in His Sermon on the Mount in Matthew chapters 5–7, *'Blessed are you when people insult you, persecute you and falsely say all kinds of evil against you because of me. Rejoice and be glad, because great is your* reward in heaven, for in the same way they persecuted the prophets who were before you' (Matthew 5:11–12). He added in Matthew 5:44–45, *'Love your enemies, bless those who curse you, do good to those who hate you, and pray for those who persecute you, that you may be sons of your Father in heaven.'* It is in responding like this to opposition that the on-looking world can see that you have been 'born again' and now, through saving faith in Jesus, know God the Father as your own Heavenly Father! Stay close to God and show the family likeness!

Fifth, if you have that saving faith ...

If you have that saving faith in the Lord Jesus Christ, please be encouraged to share your faith in Christ with other people wisely and graciously and as the opportunities arise. If you are not yet saved, remember the answer given by imprisoned Paul and Silas to the jailer in Philippi, who asked what he must do 'to be saved.' Their reply was clear, 'Believe in the Lord Jesus, and you will be saved' (Acts 16:30–31).

Soldiers Slandering

LUKE 23:26–38 (NIV)
ALSO REFER TO: MATTHEW 27:26–31; MARK 15:16–20; JOHN 19:16–24, 28–37

Jesus is crucified between the two criminals

We now focus on the soldiers on duty when Jesus died on the cross as recorded in Luke chapter 23:26–38. (Please also read the verses on the soldiers in Matthew, Mark and John, to find some added details, mentioned below.) After a cruel flogging, Jesus is led away. The soldiers make Simon of Cyrene carry His cross. They lead out two criminals to be crucified, where they flank Jesus in the centre. Barabbas should have been there.

Is Jesus willing to forgive the cruel soldiers?

I suggested earlier that the loving and compassionate words of Jesus from the cross, *'Father, forgive them, for they do not know what they are doing'*, might apply to everyone, or might have been for the religious leaders, or perhaps for the two crucified criminals, or even for the cruel, taunting, bullying, soldiers who treat Jesus so savagely and unfairly although Pilate and Herod found no case to answer. They certainly need to have their sins forgiven.

Sham coronation and copycat blasphemy

Earlier, the soldiers mocked Jesus in a sham coronation using a purple robe and a crown of thorns. They mocked Him as *'King of the Jews,'* repeatedly hit Him on the head with a staff and spat on Him. They fell on their knees in mock worship, then removed the robe of purple and replaced Jesus' own clothes. This is how they prepared the innocent King of Glory, the Lord Jesus Christ, to die. They now continue that cruel mocking, offer Him sour wine vinegar, and carry on the theme of insulting the would-be king. Pilate's written notice above Jesus on His cross is: '*THIS IS THE KING OF THE JEWS.*' The soldiers' second-hand taunts copy the sneering religious rulers' words, '*He saved others; let Him save Himself if He is the Christ of God, the Chosen One.*' The soldiers' version is, '*If you are the king of the Jews, save yourself.*' Their copycat blaspheming of the eternal Son of God is now copied again by one of the prisoners. You need not be very bright to copy others' cheap anti-God and anti-Christ slogans!

Great evidence for our infallible Bible

Great evidence for God's perfect authorship of the infallible Bible is seen here, and in the other Gospels about Jesus' clothing. Combining those passages together, here is what happens: the soldiers divide up Jesus' clothing into four shares between them. It seems that four soldiers and their Centurion are on crowd control around those three crosses. (We will meet the Centurion later.) No doubt he can call for more men, if needed. We read in John 19:23–24 that there is a seamless undergarment made in one piece, and presumably good quality. The soldiers agree not to tear that up but to cast lots for it. As they do so, they unwittingly fulfil a part of a prophecy of Scripture, Psalm 22:16–18, which prophesies that on the cross Jesus will be surrounded, His hands and feet will be pierced, His bones will stick out (as He hangs extended on that cross), He will be looked at and stared at, and that while some of His clothing will be divided, other clothing will be taken by casting lots. Even the miserable actions of the soldiers were recorded in prophecy hundreds of years before crucifixion was practised in Israel.

Why break the legs of crucified men?

Also, they often broke the legs of crucified dying victims in the later stages of crucifixion to stop them pushing up against the downward pressure impacting their chests, which would eventually cause suffocation. The soldiers therefore break the legs of both weakened and dying criminals to cause them to die earlier. But when they get to Jesus, they find Him dead already. This fulfils Old Testament Scriptures that none of His bones will be broken (Exodus 12:46; Numbers 9:12; Psalm 34:20). Of course, Jesus did not persuade them before not to break His legs to fulfil Old Testament prophecy! He is already dead when they come to break His legs. All this is further evidence that God's inspired prophecy in the Bible is nothing less than history told by God through the prophets in advance! We really can trust the Bible!

Lessons to learn

We can learn much from what happens around and through these soldiers:

It was vital that Jesus should die

The soldiers are there to ensure that all the victims of crucifixion die on their crosses—including Jesus. Remember why it is vital for Jesus to die on that cross and rise again three days later. He is sinless and perfect and is punished there for us by God the Father, to take the judgment and penalty we deserve for all our sins. Only when we turn from those sins and by faith give our lives to Jesus, shall we escape Hell, know our sins are forgiven, and gain a home forever in Heaven. God also changes and blesses us now as we become what Jesus called 'born again' spiritually! Jesus had to die.

Did Jesus really die?

Some sceptics from various religions, or because they reject the Bible as God's word, say that Jesus did not really die on the cross but swooned, and so his resurrection was a fake. There are some very strong reasons why they are wrong. But just for now, remember these hard soldiers are professional 'crucifiers.' They know their job: their futures and even their lives depend on them doing it well. They all know the two criminals were alive, but Jesus was dead. To prove that was so, one soldier thrusts a spear into Jesus' side, and out comes 'blood and water.' The 'water' was probably the fluid in Jesus' extended pericardial sack around his heart, and shows that, medically speaking, Jesus died of acute heart failure. This was the view of the late Professor Verna Wright, an eminent physician who often contributed medical articles in medical journals such as the Lancet. Professor Wright was the regular medical expert on a panel of various experts in their fields who discussed the evidence for the resurrection of the Lord Jesus Christ.

But please also note that Pilate double checks with the Centurion that Jesus is dead. That occurs only after Joseph of Arimathea, who obviously knew He was dead, asked Pilate's permission to put Jesus' body in his unused tomb. So did Nicodemus, a Jewish leader, who accompanied him (Mark 15:38–39). Were four professional soldiers, their experienced Centurion boss, Joseph, Nicodemus and Pilate *all* wrong? No! This theory of straw fails on various other serious grounds, too.

You can trust the Bible!

Remember the fulfilled prophecies of Scripture involving the soldiers. We considered them about and around what happened on the cross. Gallup, the American statistician is well known for the 'Gallup-polls' which accompany many elections. He said he had proved God mathematically by working out the statistical probability of a limited number of prophecies coming true, using the law of probabilities. The result of his calculations was overwhelmingly in favour of his conclusion that God exists and knows what He predicted accurately. It is foolish not to trust the Bible.

Do not abuse authority

If ever, like these soldiers, you are in a position of strength, trust and authority over others, do not abuse it. And do not pick on someone you see who you think is in a weaker position than you are. Abuse and bullying are wrong and sinful, and God will judge it if it is not confessed and forsaken.

Never give in to peer pressure

Have you ever wondered if at least one of the soldiers did not really agree at heart with what his colleagues were doing, but was scared to say so? If so, he should nevertheless have objected and refused to take part. Never give in to peer pressure, hard as that can be. If you trust Jesus, you will find He gives you courage.

Don't cover up your ignorance by mocking

Never mock something just because you do not understand it and find it easier to laugh at it than think it all through. Keep quiet and humbly find out what it is all about.

Think things through for yourself

Make sure that any objections you raise to something are not just other people's second-hand objections, or something you are saying to please others, or to look clever. Think things through for yourself: then object if you are sure your cause is important, worthy and justified.

'The Son of God loved me and gave Himself for me'

Finally, please reflect again on how much Jesus loved you to go through all He suffered on the cross, when He died for you, bearing your sins. Think of 'the Son of God, who loved me and gave Himself for me' (Galatians 2:20). If you have not already repented and trusted in Jesus, make sure that, as a point or urgency, you do turn from your sins and ask Him into your life as your Saviour. Determine to put Him first in your life each day, as your Lord, and tell Him so. Pray to Him each day and read some of His word, the Bible, daily and carefully. And make sure you get regular fellowship and worship with other Christians each week.

Obstinate offender

LUKE 23:32–34 (NIV)
ALSO REFER TO: LUKE 23:39–43; MATTHEW 27:38; JOHN 19:17–18; MARK 15:27, 32;
JOHN 19:31–3; ISAIAH 53:9–12

The criminal who was not converted

In Chapter 6, we looked at the *'Criminal converted.'* We also met his partner in crime, as both were in the same gang. The boss of that gang was Barabbas, a murderer, robber, and the leader of violent public disorders. Now we examine that second criminal who died alongside Jesus. I call him, an *'Obstinate offender.'* Actually, very little is said about him, but the silence is a deafening warning of the tragedy of not turning from sin to trust in Jesus. This book is mainly based on Luke chapter 23. But please read the quotes included from the other Gospels and from Chapter 53 of the Old Testament prophet, Isaiah who, through the Holy Spirit, predicted Jesus' substitutionary death on the cross for and with sinners.

This guilty man initially joined with his criminal colleague, the *'Criminal converted' in* Chapter 6, to insult Jesus. But as time went on his companion stopped insulting and blaspheming and turned to Jesus with a personal plea to the eternal Son of God, 'Jesus, remember me when You come into Your kingdom.' Jesus told him he would be with Him that very day in Paradise. You may recall that the newly converted offender rebuked the man whom we are considering now. He was warned not to reject Jesus.

Never too late to come—but some leave it too late

This Bible event is the one I like best to preach on in Chaplaincy services in HM Prisons and Immigration Removal Centres. It shows how the Lord Jesus Christ knows all about, loves, hears, and answers the prayers of any prisoners anywhere who call humbly upon Him. He will save anyone who repents from ('turns his back upon') sin itself and therefore from being judged and punished everlastingly with the judgment of Hell. We rightly tell people that it is never too late to come humbly to Jesus, to confess their sins from the heart, and ask Him to save them and enter into their lives as their personal Saviour.

Where is the 'obstinate offender' now?

But we do need also to tell them where his associate is now spending eternity, and why that is. It is true that, while you are alive, it is never too late to come to Christ to receive His pardon and new life within you. But it is equally true that you can leave it too late to come. Sometimes, you miss the moment and may not feel the same way again and never take that step of faith. Or you can say 'No' to the invitation of Jesus once too often. Your heart can get so hardened that it can no longer hear that merciful voice of Jesus in your soul urging you to repent and look to the cross, where Jesus bore all your sins and their punishment in your place, so you will not be punished. Or maybe you are aware of your need to come to Jesus, but you simply will not come because you think the cost is too high. You cannot go your own selfish and sinful way anymore when you repent—which means being so sorry for your sins that you turn from them—and ask the Lord Jesus Christ into your life, as your Lord and Saviour.

What stops you turning to Christ?

If you trust Jesus as your Lord and Saviour, you have to follow and obey Him. Perhaps the cost you worry about is what others may say and think about you and your decision to live for Jesus, and make Him known, even to your friends. They may be the ones you really do not want to cross or upset. Or perhaps there is a 'pet sin,' or a collection of 'pet sins,' that simply must go if Jesus saves you and takes over. Yet you enjoy these sins or have given in to them. The Bible does tell you that it is possible 'to enjoy the pleasures of sin,' and some quote that to justify continuing in their sins, but they forget that the full quotation refers to enjoying the pleasures of sin *for a short time* (Hebrews 11:25). Hell is everlasting, and so is your lost soul. Better to face the cost of becoming a Christian, seek God's help and that of other people you might know who have trusted Jesus and follow Him, than to have these passing 'pleasures' and be lost forever.

No logical answer to the question

Is it not better to pay *any* cost rather than spending forever and ever in the conscious awareness and pain of God's eternal punishment in Hell? Once there, you can never escape. Your only means of escape is *now*, through turning to Jesus and giving your life to Him. And the *huge* bonus is that Heaven is also everlasting, and full of perfect unending joy, peace and presence of the Lord Jesus Christ with you. The Lord Jesus asks, in Mark 8:36, 'What *good is it for a* man to gain the whole world, yet forfeit his soul?' Do you have any logical answer to that? If so, you will be the first person in history to have one.

Role model

God is very gracious even to those who act, talk and scheme against Him. He constantly reminds them of the *pressing need* to turn to Jesus for forgiveness. As we have seen, even here, the criminal who gets converted reminds his former crony that they are both guilty. There is no answer to that: ignore it and be judged. But just as God gives one criminal the chance to turn to Him and be saved, so He tells the other one, through the words of his pal, that he is guilty and so needs forgiveness through trusting Jesus. The newly saved criminal is even a role model for and an example to his rebellious friend about how to be forgiven by Jesus. He is a role model for you and me also. Like him, realise that Jesus is God in flesh, the Lord Himself, and that He died to forgive you. Admit your sins to God and be prepared to resist going with what others want. Ask Him to give you a godly determination to live for Him, just as the converted man stops blaspheming and insulting Jesus. And pray a sincere prayer to the Lord and mean it. Jesus always answers prayers like that.

No middle way

But the second criminal seems to remain tragically obstinate. There is no hint or record that he did turn from his wrongdoing to ask Jesus to remember him too. If that is a correct deduction, bearing in mind that he will have died soon after the soldiers broke his and his converted friend's legs, then he was not forgiven, did not receive eternal life, was not in Paradise with his saved friend, and is eternally separate from God in Hell. There is no middle way—just a well populated broad road leading to continual eternal destruction, and a narrow way on which few travel but which is wide enough to take all true believers in Christ to Heaven (Matthew 7:13–14).

Important confirmation

Finally, both the criminals unknowingly take part in a piece of important forensic evidence. It shows that Jesus really died. The Centurion came to break their legs, so that they could not push up on them to take that vital gulp of air as they, like other victims of crucifixion, were dying from suffocation. The Centurion examined Jesus, intending to break His legs too. But when he got to Jesus, he found He was dead already. Some people deny the Bible's truth or accuracy. One religion claims Jesus did not die but swooned. Please remember that we saw that four very experienced Roman soldiers and their Centurion knew He was dead, as did Joseph of Arimathea and Nicodemus. And Governor Pilate made sure by having the Centurion check it out again, which he did.

The value of Jesus' death accepted showed in the resurrection
There is no doubt that Jesus did die, and that He rose again from the dead. That was how God the Father showed He was satisfied with the value of Jesus' death to save guilty repentant sinners like us who put our trust in Him. We have a once crucified, now risen, Saviour God. Trust Him now with all your heart!

Centurion seeking

LUKE 23:44–47 (NIV)
ALSO REFER TO: MARK 15:33–39, 44–45

The Roman Centurion in charge

Our attention now is drawn to the Roman Centurion in charge. There are various Roman Centurions we read of in the Bible. The Romans worshipped multi-gods, as well as the only LORD God of Scripture. Most Centurions will be as ignorant and confused about how to come to know God as other people are. But some Centurions we meet in the Bible seem really serious about the Lord Jesus Christ. Hopefully some turn from their sins to Christ, become 'saved,' and so love and obey Him. Others seem to be seekers: remember that Jesus said, *'seek and you will find'* (Matthew 7:7).

The Centurion at the cross of Jesus

This man is remembered as the Centurion at the cross of Jesus. He reminds us that whatever you might have done or believed, or whatever your background has been or is, or however influential you have been or are, that you personally need Jesus. Because you need Him, just turn to Him for forgiveness and receive eternal life. The Lord Jesus Christ died on the cross for you, took the punishment for your sins there, and rose again from the dead to be your Saviour. He will enter your life and change you if you do an about turn from going your own way—including your sins—and receive Him in your life personally as your Lord and Saviour.

No quick path to becoming a Centurion

A Roman Centurion commanded 100 (or a 'century' of) men. In practice sometimes it was as few as eighty. I suppose that depended largely on how many men had been lost in battles and where the soldiers were stationed. Approximately a thousand men made up a cohort. Between 3,000 and 6,000 men (thirty to sixty cohorts) constituted a Roman Legion. There was no quick path to becoming a Centurion: the right to promotion was earned when a man showed he was a good and reliable soldier, with leadership qualities and undoubted bravery. He came up the 'hard way' through the ranks. He might have been injured in battle. He would prove himself as a hard and brave man, who also knew how to lead and inspire his troops. He was not a man to compromise easily on anything 'shaky' or doubtful! He would not 'suffer fools gladly.'

Sequence of events

This Centurion is on duty, overseeing his men, at the crucifixions of Jesus and the criminals, one on each side of Jesus. He probably is responsible for all the other crucifixions taking place at the time, as is common under Roman rule in Jerusalem. Put together Luke 23:44–47 and Mark 15:33–45 and you get the sequence of remarkable events that this Centurion will witness, or know about, as he stands 'there in front of Jesus' crucified on His cross.

Mid-day darkness, and veil torn

First, complete darkness for three hours starts at mid-day (the same as their 'sixth hour'), and when the overhead sun is always at its brightest. This goes on till 3 pm (the 'ninth hour'). At the same time as the sun fails to shine, the multi-layered veil of the temple (as thick as a man's fist) is torn in two, from top to bottom. That veil separates God's presence, in the 'Holy of holies,' from the surrounding holy place. It signifies that sinful man is separated from holy God by his sin. It is torn from God's side (the top) to man's side (the bottom). Its tearing is a picture that the way to God is now open because Christ died to bear the sins of those who trust Him and take their punishment on the cross. That is why, today also, you can come to Christ. Jesus rose and is alive. If you trust in Him,

He will enter your heart and life and change you from within. He has broken down the barrier of sin. All who repent and trust Him find fellowship with God now and can enter Heaven's Glory confidently after death.

Two of Christ's cries from the cross

Before the darkness fell and the veil was torn, the Centurion hears Jesus crying out from the cross. Two cries are mentioned here—there were five other cries too. The first cry the Centurion hears is, *'My God, my God, why have you forsaken me?'* The second 'loud cry,' before Jesus breathes His last breath, is *'Father, into your hands I commit my spirit.'* No-one took His life from Jesus: He laid it down Himself when He knew that He had fully paid the penalty for our sins. Is the most impressive thing to the Centurion, that Jesus is in charge even of the timing of His horrible death, and that He dies with such dignity?

Another cry: 'It is finished!'

Another earlier cry is, *'It is finished!'* (John 19:30). It is a huge cry of triumph. A similar victory cry was shouted by a victorious gladiator after battling hard for his life in the amphitheatre. It signalled he had overcome the opponent or wild animal he was forced to fight. It means, 'It is accomplished!'

Of course, that is exactly what Jesus did accomplish when He died on the cross. He conquered sin, death, and judgment. It would take an unrepentant sinner an eternity in Hell to pay for his sins. He would suffer both death and judgment (Hebrews 9:27). Jesus paid for sin in full by shedding His own blood. Because He proclaims, 'It is finished!' I rejoice to know that my sin has been paid for in full by Him, even though I feel bad that my sins caused Him to die. I am forgiven completely and always. My sins are paid for by Jesus. Are yours?

Can a man with zero Bible background really understand the gospel?

Remember that we are not looking at a Jewish expert in Old Testament theology! We are looking at a hardened soldier from Rome who has been brought up to believe in many gods—some very immoral and obviously wicked. We cannot expect him to know or understand God's word, can we? Not unless the same Holy Spirit, who revealed Jesus as the loving Saviour who died to take sinners with Him to His Kingdom in Paradise to one of the dying criminals, is also at work. But the Holy Spirit clearly *is* at work like that in this Centurion's heart. This man with zero 'Bible background' simply stands before Jesus on the cross, takes in quietly what he sees and hears, and thinks humbly about it before God. Maybe he also prays for help to understand, or somehow senses God's presence there? We do not know. What we do know is that he now possesses and openly proclaims two truths about Jesus that we all need to take on board. Many so-called theologians even fall at these two hurdles of Jesus Christ's sinlessness and deity!

Jesus—the 'righteous man' and 'the Son of God'

He has taken in the meaning of Jesus' last cry—and may be the other cries Jesus made too. He has also seen '*how Jesus died.*' He knows Jesus has really died. He is so sure that he confirms it to Pilate who carefully checks up on what he says (Mark 15:44). He comes to his faith by thinking about Jesus and his very real death on the cross. Those are excellent ways to come to trust in Christ. But he realises two other things as well. This Roman Centurion is now convinced Jesus was a sinless '*righteous man*' (Luke 23:44), and the eternal '*Son of God*' (Mark 15:47).

The Lord Jesus Christ is unique—trust in Him

You can understand that Jesus needed to be entirely and perfectly a 'righteous man' in order to pay for our sins. If He was a sinner, He would have needed forgiveness Himself! A sinlessly perfect and completely pure sacrifice was needed to bear our sins and their punishment in His body on the cross. Jesus also had to be the *eternal* God so His sacrifice on the cross could cleanse all sins *forever*—past, present and future, for all people who turn from sin, trust in and submit to Jesus. He was and is the eternal 'Son of God.' If He had not been God in the flesh, then so much of what He said and did would be blasphemy. The Centurion got that right too! No religious leader in any of the world's religions was, or claimed to be, either completely 'righteous' and sinless, or God by nature. Jesus is unique. Is all your faith in this 'righteous man,' the eternal 'Son of God,' the Lord Jesus Christ? If not, turn from sin and trust Him now. He *will* receive you!

Culpable crowd

LUKE 23:27, 48–49 (NIV)
ALSO REFER TO: MATTHEW 27:46–52; MARK 15:29–30, 33–38; JOHN 19:19–22

What the 'murderous mob' did not know

In Chapter 3 we considered the 'murderous mob' who, whipped up by hypocritical religious leaders, were crying for innocent Jesus to be crucified. Some of that mob would be in the crowd now to watch Jesus and the two criminals, flanking Him, die on their crosses. They did not know—as we know now—that He died there to bear our sins and take God the Father's punishment in His body on that cross. The gospel depends on that. One hymn puts it like this:

Because the sinless Saviour died
my sinful heart is counted free,
for God the Just is satisfied
to look on Him and pardon me.[1]

Who make up the 'culpable crowd'?

The 'culpable crowd' we feature now is *not* exactly the same as that mob. It seems that this 'culpable crowd' consists of at least some of the following:

- Some of that 'murderous mob'—we do not know how many.
- Hostile religious leaders who try to influence the crowd against Jesus.
- Most of the individuals we meet in each chapter of Part One of this book—some for Jesus and some against Him.
- The 'large number of people' who follow Jesus to the cross (Luke 23:27), perhaps including some of the 'mourning women.'

- Some passers-by, some who met Jesus before, some who heard Him preach and teach, and/or saw some of His miracles.
- Some secret admirers of Jesus, who hate what is happening but who are too scared to say anything that may get them into trouble.
- Others who want a cheap thrill like those who watched the Reformers being burned at the stake for their faith, or victims being beheaded during the French Revolution.
- Yet others who genuinely have not made up their minds about Jesus and want to see His response to such an ordeal and death.
- Finally, just a lot of 'ordinary' folks, who happen to be there.

Why is the crowd 'culpable?'

Why call them the *'culpable* crowd?' 'Culpable' means 'to be blamed.' Why are they to be 'blamed?' The reasons may vary from person to person and from group to group, as we will see shortly. But most were 'culpable' because, having observed all that went on around that cruel cross, they failed to respond by repenting of their sins and asking God to forgive and save them. They watched Jesus die with such bravery, integrity, dignity, compassion, love and control. The evidence is that it causes them to pass that 'culpable' verdict on themselves! As Luke 23:48 states: *'When all the people who had gathered* to witness this sight saw what took place, they beat their breasts and went away.'* Beating your breast showed your remorse and anguish for your sin. Jesus told of a much-despised tax collector who beat his breast, as God convicted him of his sin. He prayed, *'God, be merciful to me a sinner'* (Luke 18:13). Jesus said he was accepted by God because he was sincere about his sin, unlike a boasting religious man, a Pharisee, who wrongly thought he was fine as he was.

Remorse or repentance?

Many in the crowd seem to decide they are sinful and unworthy too. They beat their breasts and return home in *'remorse and anguish.'* *'Remorse and anguish'* can lead toward repentance, but they fall short of repentance: that is, being so sorry for my sin that I confess it to God, turn from it, ask for mercy, and give my life to Jesus in prayer.

Why do some in the crowd not respond positively to the gospel?

Perhaps the reason why the crowd members remain culpable is because of one or more of the following factors?

1. They do not believe or want to believe what Jesus said, or what the clear key Old Testament prophecies they had heard or read say about Him.
2. They never bother even to consider the words of Jesus or those biblical prophecies seriously. What an insult to God!
3. They believe they should turn from their sins and trust Jesus as their Saviour, but they put it off and never 'get round to it.'
4. Their fear of non-Christian opposition exceeds their willingness to believe, trust and follow the Lord Jesus Christ as their Lord and Saviour.
5. They fall to anti-Jesus 'peer pressure:' it is easier to 'go with the flow' and follow the crowd, even though that broad way will lead them to Hell forever.
6. They are too occupied with this world's fears, worries and materialism.

But has the 'culpable crowd 'done us a favour?'

But, in a sad way, this crowd has 'done us a favour.' It encourages us to evaluate our response to the Lord Jesus Christ independently and be ready to fly in the face of the potential influence of the majority crowd. The Bible says, in Proverbs 29:25, *'Fear of man will prove to be a snare, but whoever trusts in the LORD is kept safe.'* Never follow the crowd or do things because many others do. The right alternative is to be someone who *'trusts in the LORD.'* Beware of falling for conscious or unconscious 'peer pressure.' *'Trust in the LORD with all your heart and lean not on your own understanding; in all your ways acknowledge Him, and He will make your paths straight'* (Proverbs 3:5–6). God's word is your map of life, and the Holy Spirit is your Guide in line with that map if you know Jesus as your personal and living Saviour. In that case, you are living to please Him, not the crowd.

The lonely path

At times it is hard to take a path of lonely obedience to Christ when so many are telling you to go another way. But if you honour the Lord, He will surely honour, keep and help you. Remember no one gets to Heaven by following the crowd. Only Jesus is *'the* way and the truth and the life. No one comes to the Father except through [Him]'* (John 14:6).

Two final valuable lessons

Please look at the other Bible verses given at the start of this chapter. There are two valuable lessons to learn about the crowd:

1. The crowd rarely understands or wants to understand what Jesus' words really mean or what the Bible clearly teaches. It takes a converted, praying person, who relies on the Bible and on the indwelling Holy Spirit, to understand any of God's teachings (Matthew 27:46–49; Mark 15:29–30).

2. Do not rely on 'religious people,' whatever religion they belong to, and however senior or expert they are in their religion. Get your teaching direct from God's word, the Bible. Study it, after prayer, each day and also listen to it being taught on the Lord's Day (Sunday) and during the week, if you get the opportunity to join in weekday Bible studies. Remember how the religious Jews were wrong about the Lord Jesus Christ as King (John 19:19–22).

Do not rely on anyone claiming to be a Christian unless he reads, studies, trusts, shares and promotes the Bible as God's word, and unless his life shows he is putting Jesus first.

Will God give them another chance to respond?

How many of the culpable crowd will be in Jerusalem at Pentecost, to hear the gospel preached by Peter? Surely many of them will be there, but if so, how many of them will listen, consider and trust in Jesus? I wonder!

NOTES

1 'God the Just' simply means He is 100% righteous and fair in judging.

Disciples distant

LUKE 23:44–49 (NIV)
ALSO REFER TO: MATTHEW 26:31–35, 55–56; MARK 15:40; JOHN 19:25–27

Loyal support

I remember being stirred at the funeral of a very faithful older Christian man whose life was devoted to sharing the gospel and helping other people. That included me at a particularly trying time in my life when I had been falsely accused and needed someone to talk to openly but confidentially. Jim was always a close Christian brother. He also became my very dear friend. I still miss him today, many years later. What moved my heart at his funeral was to see that all the four coffin bearers were his sons. They had loyally prayed for him, cared for him when he was alive, supported him when he was dying, and honoured him after his death. I found that extremely moving, especially as he had supported so many others.

Jesus alone as He dies

Let us think again about that cruel cross where Jesus bore our sins and their punishment—which it would take anyone an eternity to pay in Hell, if they fail to repent and ask Jesus into their lives to save them. Jesus suffered the penalty of eternal punishment in His body in three hours on Calvary's cross, as the sun ceased to shine at midday (Luke 23:44–45). Because He rose from the dead, God's word, in Hebrews 7:16, says Jesus now lives in the *'power of an indestructible life'* (NIV)—or *'endless life'* (NKJV). If you turn from your sins to trust Jesus personally, our indestructible and ever-living Saviour, you receive eternal life *now* and will *never* lose it (John 10:27–30).

Sadly, unlike my friend's faithful sons, not many of Jesus' disciples supported Him at His death. Although surrounded by a crowd, He is *alone* as He dies and bears men's insults and blasphemy and God the Father's holy wrath on our sins.

'From a distance'—'at a distance'

Now 'many *women*' watch '*from a distance*' at the cross. Only one *male* disciple, the Apostle John, is reported as being near enough to hear Jesus speak to him as he stood supporting Jesus' mother, as her Son died on the cross (John 19:25–27). Earlier, in the Garden of Gethsemane, provoked by the religious leaders, the mob came with swords and clubs to take Jesus for mock trials, flogging and then crucifixion. Matthew tells us that Peter, a leading disciple, followed '*at a distance*' to see what happened but then denied all knowledge of Jesus *three* times (see also, Luke 22:54–62). He had boasted to Jesus, '*Even if all fall away on your account, I never will*' and '*Even if I have to die with you, I will never disown you.*' But he did not boast alone: '*And all the other disciples said the same.*' (Matthew 26:31–35).

Weak made strong—but only as we live close to Jesus

It is not enough to make bold claims about our Christianity or think we have the strength *in ourselves* to follow Christ. We are weak, sinful, and prone to fail—which makes our conversion to Christ even more amazing. But we must keep close to Jesus, not follow Him '*at a distance.*' We are weak but, *by His strength* and if we abide in Him, He enables us to live differently and live for Him, despite our weaknesses and failures. But we must live close to Him in prayer, trust and obedience. Though still weak sinners, we are no longer *mastered* by sin. That is *entirely* through God's saving grace by which we trust in our strong Saviour, enjoy the Holy Spirit indwelling us, are helped by daily reading, and having confidence in the Bible. We are fed and helped as we listen to good Bible teaching and enjoy meeting together with Christians on the Lord's Day and having open fellowship with them during the week. We have so much in common with others who trust and follow Jesus. But without Christ, we can do *nothing.* Yet we rejoice that, as we keep turning from sin and yielding our lives to Jesus, we learn that *'sin shall not be your master, because you are not under law, but under grace'* (Romans 6:14).

We cannot get right with God by keeping His law or trying to keep it—we fail time and time again. His law shows us our sins so that we humbly ask for God's help and forgiveness for those sins and remember Christ is in us and with us. It is true that we are not *mastered* by sin, but we certainly are *assailed* by it and we do sin. The Bible says, *'If we claim to be without sin, we deceive ourselves and the truth is not in us. If we confess our sins, [God] is faithful and just and will forgive our sins and purify us from all unrighteousness'* (1 John 1:8–9). We need His cleansing every single day and always during the day too. We receive that cleansing each time, in sincere repentance, we come to Jesus and ask Him to forgive us and help us live for Him.

Always a few who follow

But there are always bound to be a few disciples at the cross who are less *'distant'* and more faithful than those well-known disciples who fled and did not *even* follow Jesus *'at a distance'* as Peter did before his triple denial. They simply were not even anywhere near the One they promised to follow to the end. Are you willing to be one of those few?

For Christians today, how important it is to live close to the Lord and His word each day, and to ask Him to keep us constantly close to Him. Do you ever 'fail to show up' when you should be there for Christ—not only in Sunday services and Bible studies, but if a fellow Christian suffers unfairness or abuse from others? I am *not* suggesting violent intervention—God does *not* want that—but rather, to ask God for His grace to help your fellow Christian explain what it means to know Jesus and to follow Him. Are you willing to be counted when the majority is against you and clearly non-Christian? For that you need to live near your living Lord day by day.

Four faithful women and one loyal man near the cross

Some Christian women were as near the cross as they could get—watching crucifixion close up was mainly a male thing to do. Those women's loyal and loving faithfulness puts many men to shame. Strength to follow Christ is less to do with muscles than to do with a heart that loves Jesus. Matthew 27:55–56 says that, among the 'Many women' coming to care for Jesus, are Mary Magdalene and Mary, the mother of some disciples. Salome is also identified in Mark 15:40. These three later go to the tomb (Mark 16:1). John adds another 'Mary' to this list, the wife of Clopas (John 19:25). A fourth very faithful 'Mary' is there too—Jesus' mother. Imagine how she feels to see her much loved son so wrongly treated—though she always knew He had a special task to do on earth, and that He is the Son of God, born through the Holy Spirit miraculously coming on her. But close to Jesus and His cross, with Jesus' brave mother, is just *one* male disciple, John. The women are on the edge of the crowd, but John takes Mary (or vice-versa?) nearer to crucified Jesus. As three other women join them, (John 19:25), Jesus speaks to His mother and to John. He cares for His mother by asking John to treat her like his own mother. He cares for His loving and close disciple, John, by asking Mary to act as a mother to him. What amazing love from a dying, bleeding, sin-bearing Saviour, Himself in a time of real need! John takes grieving Mary into his home (John 19:26–27).

Are you a disciple who stays close to Jesus?

Are you Jesus' disciple? Do you follow Him closely each day? Or do you just look on from afar? Perhaps you are a Christian who has let things slip, and you need to re-commit your life to Jesus?

Or maybe your greatest need is to trust Jesus as your Lord and Saviour, by asking Him into your life? You cannot be His disciple unless you know Him. And coming to know Jesus opens up a life of discipleship to the new convert. Remember that He died for you, loves you, and will bless and keep you if you trust Him. Remember, too, to keep close to Him.

Follower faithful

LUKE 23:50–54 (NIV)
ALSO REFER TO: MATTHEW 27:57–61; MARK 15:42–47; JOHN 19:38–42

Who is Joseph of Arimathea?

Several men called 'Joseph' are found in the Bible. The best-known Josephs are Jacob's son, the man with the multi-coloured coat who became the equivalent of the Prime Minister of Egypt, and the husband of Mary, Jesus' mother. Now meet another Joseph: Joseph of Arimathea in Judah. Who is he?

To answer that we will look at Joseph from each of the four Gospels' 'camera angles'—Luke 23:50–54 Matthew 27:57–61; Mark 15:42–47 and John 19:38–42. We can learn a lot from what he did and why. There are important lessons and blessings here for us all.

'Secret disciple'

Jesus died on Calvary's cross in our place to bear our sins and the punishment that we deserved. Before then, Joseph was a 'secret disciple' of Jesus. You cannot remain a 'secret disciple' for long. Either your growing inner conviction or the force of circumstances will cause you to make it known that you know and follow Jesus as your Lord and Saviour. Otherwise, you will lose your Christian edge, and perhaps backslide into sin and compromise, until you repent and come back to God to be forgiven. Then you must follow Jesus whole-heartedly. I was so miserable when I was backsliding. At times I tried to hide my wobbly faith in Christ so I could 'go with the crowd' to doubtful places for reasons that did not please God or help me. I vainly tried to fool myself that I could be a Christian at the same time. I was a hypocrite. A Christian friend challenged me by saying, 'If Jesus is not your Lord of *all*, then he is not your Lord *at all*'. Romans 14:9 says, '*For this very reason, Christ died, and*

returned to life so that He might be the Lord of both the dead and the living.'
That included *me.*

Why was Joseph a secret disciple and what changed him?

The four Gospel descriptions of him reveal at least two important things:
he is *'a member of the Council'* and he is a *'prominent member of the
Council.'* John adds he is a disciple *'secretly because he feared the Jews.'*
The 'Council' (also known as 'Sanhedrin') is the ruling supreme court of
the Jews and feared by Joseph. The crooked Chief Priest is its President.
Pharisees and Sadducees control it. Joseph, a 'rich man,' has a prominent
position. If he antagonises them, he may face strong and cruel opposition
and persecution, as other Christians soon will.

But when God works in a man, it changes how he acts. Joseph's heart
belongs to the Lord, despite his fear of the Jews holding him back from
whole-hearted discipleship. He is described as: *'a good and upright man,'*
'waiting for the kingdom of God,' who *'had himself become a disciple of
Jesus,'* (presumably when already a Council member). But things are
changing—he recently has 'not consented to their decision and action'
about crucifying Jesus. His change from secret disciple to bold witness
for Christ, seems to have begun. He rejects his Council colleagues' unjust
and cruel treatment of Jesus. Now he reaches a 'crunch point.' He now
feels compelled to show his loving support for Jesus by asking for His
dead body, soon after seeing Jesus die. God is now strengthening his
former 'secret disciple.' He now goes *'boldly to Pilate and asked for Jesus'
body.'* Pilate knows who he is. His position and influence allow him to be
bold in front of this hard and cruel Roman Governor, as he asks for Jesus'
body. His discipleship is no longer secret. He now invests his life,
reputation, and future in following Christ, as he openly identifies with
his crucified Saviour. He will now take any resultant 'flack.'

Did Joseph survive the persecution of Christians?

Does he survive the later widespread persecution of Christians that starts in Jerusalem with Stephen's martyrdom? We do not know. But he has exchanged being a 'secret disciple' to be known as a caring disciple who approaches boldly the Roman Governor, to request the body of his beloved Saviour, and generously gives his own new tomb, intended for his own burial, to bury Jesus. The best that he kept for himself is now given to His Saviour and Lord. Soon, across the world, after the well-testified resurrection of Jesus takes place from Joseph's tomb, the entire world will know that Joseph of Arimathea is on the side of the Lord Jesus Christ.

To prepare Jesus' body decently for burial (as we would want to do for our loved ones) he teams up with Nicodemus, another Council member. Nicodemus previously visited Jesus *by night* (again, probably from *'fear of the Jews'* and especially those on the Council). Jesus told him *'You must be born again'* and explained what that meant (see, John 3:3,7; compare 1 Peter 1:23). The Bible's most well-known verse, John 3:16, is the result.

So is Nicodemus, the once 'secret seeker,' now 'born again?' I *think* so. Why? Well, just like Joseph will do later, he speaks out for fair treatment of Jesus. Also, he now identifies with Joseph and Jesus, even before

Pontius Pilate, in asking for Jesus' body. (Read about Nicodemus in John 3:1–21; 7:45–52 and 19:38–42.) So, it seems that he who once feared the Jews now helps and supports his Christian Council colleague, Joseph, by working with him to honour Christ. Those God blesses want to bless others, and those converted to Christ want to help their brothers and sisters in Christ.

Blessings and lessons to receive and learn

What blessings and lessons come for us from considering Joseph of Arimathea?

- First, do you know Jesus Christ in your heart as your Lord and Saviour? Do you realise He took in His body the full judgment for your sins for you? Have you asked the risen, living Jesus into your life by the Holy Spirit's indwelling? That is the most important issue ever.

- Do you see the benefits of not being a 'secret disciple' but openly trusting, obeying, following, honouring and living for Jesus, by His grace, strength and power? Read Romans 10:9–10. When you 'believe in your heart' in Jesus and 'confess with your mouth "Jesus is Lord"' these three blessings always follow:

  1. God is pleased, honoured and obeyed (the priority).

  2. You are greatly blessed and helped by God yourself. For a start, your assurance of salvation comes from exercising saving faith in Jesus in such a real way that you are prepared to tell other people about it. When you confess Jesus as Lord to others it blesses you, and probably others in God's time.

  3. Some who see your changed conduct and hear what Jesus means to you will want to come to trust Him as their Saviour too. But remember, it is not always easy!

- Remember Joseph and Nicodemus—make sure that you enjoy fellowship and mutual help with others who know and love

Christ, and work with them when you can. Support fellow Christians. Make your 'secret' an open one to share with others.

Any change?

If you were a secret disciple of Jesus, even occasionally, when you started reading about Joseph of Arimathea are you now willing to ask God to give you the courage to make it known that you love Jesus, and reflect that in how you live? How about doing that *now*, today?

If you have not yet turned to Jesus to save you, make sure you are wholehearted when you turn from your sins to receive Him in your heart and life as your Lord.

Christ crucified

LUKE 23:34, 43–47 (NIV)
ALSO REFER TO: 1 PETER 2:24; 3:18; ISAIAH 53:4–6

The seven sayings of Jesus from the cross

The Bible records Jesus speaking seven times while He was nailed to the cross, before He died there having borne our sins and their punishment.

Those seven sayings are listed below in the order in which He spoke. We will cover this later in the chapter, but why not start this chapter by meditating on them, first: they tell us a lot about our 'Immanuel,' Lord and Saviour.

1. Luke 23:34: *'Father, forgive them, for they do not know what they are doing.'*

2. Luke 23:43: Jesus answered the repentant criminal, *'I tell you the truth, today you will be with me in paradise.'*

3. John 19:26: (Jesus) said to his mother, 'Dear woman, here is your son,' and to the disciple, 'Here is your mother.'

4. Matthew 27:46: About the ninth hour Jesus cried out in a loud voice, 'Eloi, Eloi, lama sabachthani?'—which means, 'My God, my God, why have you forsaken me?' (repeated in Mark 15:34).

5. John 19:28: Later knowing that all was now completed, and so that the Scripture would be fulfilled, Jesus said, 'I am thirsty.'

6. John 19:30: He said, 'It is finished.' With that, bowed His head and gave up His spirit.

7. Luke 23:46: Jesus called out with a loud voice, 'Father, into your hands I commit my spirit.'

The most important Person

The most important Person you can meet at the cross, or ever meet anywhere else is the Lord Jesus Christ. He is the eternal Son of God and God the Son: He came to earth to save you and me, and many others, from sin's penalty and power. He came from Heaven to earth, to be born of Mary, a godly virgin. God the Holy Spirit miraculously enabled Mary to conceive the 'God-Man' Jesus. A baby takes its nature from both its father and mother. The Holy Spirit is God, in the Trinity with God the Father and God the Son. His only *physical* child, Jesus, took the nature of God from Him and His mother's human nature from her, but unlike all others (all of whom were born with a human nature) Jesus would never sin. Also, unlike all others, He was born as fully God and fully Man at the same time. As radio waves and oxygen occupy the same air space at the same time without changing the other, Jesus Christ perfectly blended His 100% deity with His 100% humanity. As the only sinless, perfect Man, Jesus never sinned, though tempted. He lived a life perfectly in harmony with His position and character as holy God in human flesh. His other best-known New Testament name is 'Immanuel' (or 'Emmanuel') which means 'God with us' (Isaiah 7:14; Matthew 1:23).

Jesus, our sinless substitute

It is essential that Jesus is without sin. He came to die on the cross willingly to bear your sins and equally willingly to accept the eternal wrath of God the Father on them. If you bear that wrath yourself, you will spend eternity separate from God in Hell. If Jesus had ever sinned, He could never have become your perfect substitute on the cross, because He would need to be punished for His own sin. Because He had no sin, He paid the price for yours through shedding His blood there for you. He rose again from the dead on the third day: this is God the Father's way of proclaiming to a watching world that He accepts the sacrifice of Jesus on the cross as being effective to forgive you for your sins, and give you eternal life *if* you will humbly admit you are a guilty sinner, turn from your sins, and ask Jesus to enter your life as your Lord and Saviour to trust and to follow.

A Bible summary of why Jesus died

1 Peter 2:24 and 3:18 summarise well why Jesus died. Read also the whole of the prophecy about the cross in Isaiah 52:13–53:12.

1 Peter 2:24 says, '*He himself bore our sins in His body on the tree, so that we might die to sins and live for righteousness…*'

1 Peter 3:18 says, '*For Christ died for sins once for all, the righteous for the unrighteous, to bring you to God. He was put to death in the body but made alive by the Spirit.*'

Four ways that Jesus suffered on the cross

We need to remind ourselves that, as the 'Man, Christ Jesus' is nailed to the cross, He suffers in at least four ways, even though He is God as well as Man.

First, He knows that most of His closest followers and friends have forsaken Him. How would you feel if in your hour of deep and real need, the same thing happened to you?

Second, He has been terribly wounded, battered and bruised: the soldiers repeatedly hit Him on the head, the cruel scourging He suffered had itself killed some due to be crucified after it, the huge thorns on the crown pushed onto His head would add to His bleeding, He was weak from lack of sleep and found it physically hard to carry His cross all the way to Calvary (and so Simon of Cyrene was made to do it), and then He was nailed and, in the added pain of fighting suffocation, He hung upon that cross.

Third, He faced the nasty opposition and mocking of a hostile mob. Imagine how that felt. Would you like your loved ones to face their dying moments in such a hostile environment? Of course not!

Fourth, worse of all—and that is probably why God put darkness over the cross while Jesus suffered—He was not only separated from His eternal Father for the first and only time in eternity or time, but He was judged and punished by God the Father in three hours with the eternal punishment that it will take the whole of eternity to pay for anyone who does not repent and trust in Jesus. Christ's death on the cross was not only 'theological' and certainly not 'mechanical:' here is the unprecedented suffering of a perfect and sinless Person. It moves me greatly when I think that He did that *for me.*

No one Gospel contains all Jesus' seven sayings on the cross. As we saw at the start of this chapter the teaching from all the four Gospels is blended in the order in which He said them from the cross. We now consider what they are saying to us.

First, Luke 23:34: 'Father, forgive them, for they do not know what they are doing.'

Jesus is flanked by the two convicted criminals we met earlier. To start with, they insult Jesus. The soldiers bring them: they too mock Him and divide up His clothes between them. We have already asked when Jesus says, '*Father, forgive them, for they do n*ot know what they are doing,' who does He refer to as 'them?' The criminals, the soldiers, both sets of those men, the religious rulers, or the abusive crowd generally? Or maybe all of them? We are not told, but forgiveness for offending sinners is high up in the priorities of our dying Saviour. Have you turned from your sins and asked Him to forgive and save you? Christians, too, need to keep short accounts with God, and ask for His cleansing when they sin. This is not to be saved again as that happens only once in the life of each real

Christian, but to restore our on-going *fellowship* with God, where our sins have spoiled that.

Second, Luke 23:43: 'Jesus answered him, "I tell you the truth, today you will be with me in paradise."'

Do you remember the dying criminal who repented and asked the Lord, 'Jesus, remember me when you come into Your kingdom'? Do you recall Jesus' reply to him was, *'today you will be with me in paradise'*? With a heart sorry for sin, and understanding that Jesus was dying for him, he prayed simply, *'Remember me.'* He gained His place in Heaven simply because sinless Jesus loved him and bore his sins and their penalty on the cross in his place. Have you prayed simply and personally to Jesus like that? The words you say are important, but not nearly as important as having a heart that is sorry for sinning against God and that is humble enough to ask for forgiveness and surrender to the Lord Jesus Christ.

Third, John 19:26: 'When Jesus saw his mother there, and the disciple who Jesus loved standing nearby, he said to his mother, "Dear woman, here is your son," and to the disciple [John], "Here is your mother."'

Jesus was concerned both for His close family—none closer than His mother—and for John, a disciple He loved. Dying there, His concern for them was greater than for Himself. John promptly and unselfishly took Mary into his family home. How unselfish are you? Do you care well for your family? Do you care about their relationships with God?

Fourth, Matthew 27:46: 'My God, my God, why have you forsaken me?'

We now see *'the one mediator between God and men, the man Christ Jesus'* (1 Timothy 2:5) respond in His humanity to the horror of separation from His Father as He becomes our sin-bearer. He is forsaken, abandoned, smitten, judged and punished for us on the cross. To bear Hell's eternal punishment in three hours of darkness on the cross is entirely beyond our understanding. Here is Jesus, the human being, showing the pain of separation from God the Father. And it was our sins that caused it.

Fifth, John 19:28: 'Later knowing that all was now completed, and so that the Scripture would be fulfilled, Jesus said, "I am thirsty."'

See Jesus suffer as a man. His cruel ordeals make him thirst while He endures trials, cruel flogging, little sleep, being nailed to the cross, and all alone bearing our sins. Hell is a thirsty place, too. The rich man *'in agony in this fire'* craved for water to *'cool [his] tongue'* (Luke 16:24).

Sixth, John 19:30: 'After receiving the sour wine, Jesus said, "It is finished." 'With that, he bowed his head and gave up his spirit.'

The finished work of Christ means that Jesus has done *all* there is to do to save a lost Hell-bound sinner who repents and trusts in Him alone to save him. Jesus *guarantee*s that person a place in Heaven. 'Finished' means 'completed' or 'accomplished.' You can neither add to, nor take from, Christ's finished work on the cross. It is done and is settled *forever*. So, trust in Him alone.

Seventh, Luke 23:46 'Father, into your hands I commit my spirit.'

It is at this point that John 19:30 tells us, *'With that He bowed His head and gave up His spirit.'* Battered and bleeding Jesus is nevertheless in control. He commits Himself to His Father, bows His head, and then gives up His spirit. Even at this time, He is in charge of His timetable. Always able to escape, He chose to suffer like this to save you and me.

'Were you there when they crucified my Lord?'

The words of this moving hymn ask if *you* were 'there' when Jesus died on the cross. Obviously, you were not there physically, but do you see Him dying there in *your* place for your sins? Spiritually, have *you* been to Calvary's cross to ask for forgiveness, as *you* turn from *your* sins and receive Christ in *your* life to be *your* Lord? It would be a tragedy to know that Jesus died there for you but fail to repent of your sins and ask Him to become *your* Lord and Saviour.

Sovereign satisfied

LUKE 23:44–46 (NIV)
ALSO REFER TO: MATTHEW 27:45–54; MARK 15:33–39; JOHN 19:28–37; ISAIAH
52:13–53:12; 1 PETER 2:21–25; 3:18

Recap on those we have met who witnessed Jesus' crucifixion

In Part 1 of this book we have 'met' fourteen different people and groups who were at or around the cross of the Lord Jesus Christ when He died for their and our sins. We have focused on Pilate, Barabbas (who was possibly there), the mob, Simon of Cyrene, the women, the crucified criminal who trusted Jesus, the religious rulers, the soldiers, the crucified criminal who did not turn to Jesus, the Centurion, the crowd at the cross, the disciples, Joseph of Arimathea, and the Lord Jesus Christ Himself.

The cross as God the Father sees it

Now we look at the cross as the Bible says God the Father sees it. Well, how *does* our almighty Sovereign Lord view the cross? We can imagine how a God of love felt when His beloved Son willingly died in the place of guilty sinners. But now we will look at the Gospel accounts in Matthew 27:45–54; Mark 15:33–38 and John 19:28–37 to see how God *intervened* at the cross, and then see what the Bible says about it.

The big question is, *'Is God satisfied with the sacrifice Jesus made at Calvary's cross to save sinners, like us, from sin's penalty in Hell, sin's power in life, and sin's presence in Heaven?* We also see how God inspired the prophet Isaiah to write about Jesus' death 600 years before crucifixion came to Israel (via occupation by the Romans, for whom crucifixion was their standard method of execution). We will finally see in 1 Peter 2:21–25 and 3:18 how Peter, inspired by the Holy Spirit, applies in his letter that prophecy of Jesus' death on the cross.

Five questions

In Luke 23:44–46 we learn that the sun is blotted out of the whole land from 9 am (*'the sixth hour'*) to 12 Noon (*'the ninth hour'*).

QUESTION ONE: WHO DID THAT?

Then, after the *'sun stopped shining,'* as Jesus dies, the temple curtain is torn in two from top to bottom. The 'curtain' (or 'veil') is multi-layered and multi-coloured, each colour having biblical significance, and, as I have already mentioned, is as thick as a man's fist. The fact it is torn from the top (God's position) to the bottom (man's position) signifies that the way into the temple's holiest place, the 'Holy of Holies,' is now open to *everyone.* That tearing comes after Jesus commits His spirit to His Father and then breathes His last.

QUESTION TWO: WHO ARRANGED THAT TIMING AND TORE THE CURTAIN FROM THE TOP TO THE BOTTOM TO GIVE US ACCESS TO GOD?

Matthew 27:45–54 and Mark 15:33–38 confirm Luke's account. Matthew adds that when Jesus died other remarkable, miraculous events occurred: *'The earth shook and the rocks split.'*

QUESTION THREE: WHO DID THAT?

Then, when *'The tombs broke open'* dead *'holy people'* were *'raised to life'* and appeared to people in Jerusalem after Jesus' resurrection.

QUESTION FOUR: WHO MADE THAT HAPPEN?

These things are not done in secret or in a quiet corner; they are witnessed by a large and mixed crowd. Some are Christian believers. Others have no belief in Christ. The Roman Centurion and his guarding soldiers are terrified. They conclude that Jesus is *'a righteous man'* (Luke 23:47). In both Matthew 27:54 and Mark 15:39 the same Centurion also recognises Jesus as *'the Son of God.'* Jesus is both God in the flesh and the only ever sinlessly perfect man. He is the only one the world has ever known to meet *either* of those descriptions. He is *both* at the same time.

QUESTION FIVE: WHO REVEALED THOSE IMPORTANT TWIN TRUTHS ABOUT JESUS'
SIMULTANEOUS DEITY AND HUMANITY TO PREVIOUSLY PAGAN ROMANS?

The only possible answer to all those five questions is 'God.'

God is telling the watching world that Jesus' death is special

In effect, God is telling the watching world, at a time when Jerusalem is
packed with people who witness what happens, that there is something
very special indeed about the death of Jesus on that cruel Roman cross.
God obviously knows all about it and wants Christ's death on the cross
to be marked and never to be forgotten. We can safely deduce that these
well-known miraculous acts we just shared reveal that God is fully
satisfied with the work accomplished on the cross by Jesus. Remember
that Jesus is God the Son. He is one with God the Father and with God the
Holy Spirit in the Trinity of Three Persons-in-One-God and One-God-
in-Three-Persons.

Eternity is a simple concept for our eternal God!

We should expect God to be fully involved in this unique way. Revelation
13:8 says that Jesus is *'the Lamb slain from the foundation of the world.'*
Long before our Immanuel, or *'God with us,'* became the virgin Mary's
baby at Bethlehem after the Holy Spirit came upon her, He is regarded as
'slain from the foundation of the world.'

The concept of eternity is not an easy one to grasp with our mere
earthly human minds, even though we are informed by God's infallible
truth in the Bible. But it is clearly always in God's mind, for whom
eternity is a simple concept. It is also in His eternal plan that Jesus will
become that sacrificial lamb of whom John the Baptist said, *'Look, the
Lamb of God, who takes away the sin of the world!'* At the baptism of Jesus,
as God the Holy Spirit came *'as a dove'* and remained on Him, God the
Father said to John, *'Look, the Lamb of God.'* So, the death of Christ on
the cross is not an afterthought or the best God can make out of a bad

situation. It is God's plan from eternity to save all those who will trust in, and therefore be saved by, personal faith in Christ.

How it works out in practice

How does it work out in practice, in the light of the amazing prophecy in Isaiah 52:13–53:12? (Please read that carefully in full.) The parts of Isaiah 53:4–6, emphasised below, show what God the Father is expecting Jesus to do when, as Isaiah 53:3 says, *'He was despised and rejected by men, a man of sorrows, and familiar with suffering,'* as He hung nailed to that cross:

4 Surely he took up our infirmities and carried our sorrows, yet we considered him stricken by God, smitten by him, and afflicted. 5 But he was pierced for our transgressions, he was crushed for our iniquities; the punishment that brought us peace was upon him, and by his wounds we are healed. 6 We all, like sheep, have gone astray, each of us has turned to his own way; and the LORD has laid on him the iniquity of us all.

1 Peter 2:24 speaks of Jesus and shows what Isaiah's prophecy means: *'He himself bore our sins in his body on the tree, so that we might die to sins*

and live for righteousness; by his wounds you have been healed.' As Jesus bears our sins in His body on the cross (referred to here as the 'tree') it is then that He is *'stricken by God, smitten by Him ... pierced for our iniquities,'* and that He bears the *'punishment that brought us peace ... upon Him.'* We are 'healed' not of physical ailments (or else a Christian going to the cross for forgiveness could never be ill again, which is just not so) but we are 'healed forever' of effects of the dread and deadly disease of our sin that is punished in Christ on that cross. Had that not been the case, we would be in Hell paying eternally for our own sins. God's cure, His *spiritual* healing, brings us His total forgiveness, peace with Him, and His peace in our hearts. This is all because '*the* LORD [God] *has laid on Him* [Jesus] *the iniquity of us all,*' when on the cross our Sovereign (the Lord Jesus Christ), becomes our Substitute, our Sin-bearer and our Saviour. To be saved eternally now, and escape Hell to gain Heaven, you must repent of your sins, trust fully that you have forgiveness and eternal life only because Jesus died on the cross in your place taking your punishment and receive Him in your heart as your risen and ever-living Saviour and Lord. 1 Peter 3:18 summarises the result of all this very well: '*Christ died for sins once for all, the righteous for the unrighteous, to bring you to God.*'

Jesus fulfils the Father's will for Him *perfectly*. As a sinless and spotlessly perfect sacrifice He takes the punishment as judgment for our sins that we deserve. That must satisfy the Father. 1 John 1:7 says, '*the blood of Jesus, His Son, purifies us from all sin.*' 1 John 1:9 tells us how: '*If we confess our sins,* [directly to Him through Jesus], *He is faithful and just and will forgive us our sins and purify us from all unrighteousness.*' In order to do that, God shows us that He is more than satisfied with Jesus' sacrifice of Himself on the cross to save us, by marking it with the miraculous happenings we have already seen in this chapter.

An even more amazing proof that God accepts Jesus' work on the cross

There is another even more amazing, miraculous, and extremely well-attested event that shows that God the Father and God the Holy Spirit are well satisfied with God the Son's sacrifice of Himself to save us. It is the resurrection of the Lord Jesus Christ from the dead. We will consider this in Part 2 of this book, under the title 'Were You There ... When He Rose Up From The Grave?'

But briefly for now, the Bible says that God raised Jesus from the dead in His miraculous resurrection. He would not have done that if Christ's sacrifice had been insufficient, or if Jesus had sinned or failed. The resurrection tells us that the death of Christ for our sins is the most valuable and *only* currency that can ever be accepted in Heaven. We will be there, only because He died for sinners, with our once crucified and slain, but now resurrected and ever-living Saviour and Lord, Jesus Christ!

The evidence is all there—you need no more!

All these miraculous but well-attested facts, even apart from the key evidence of the resurrection of Jesus from that secured tomb, tell us that God the Father accepts the sacrifice of the Saviour, Jesus, in payment as the penalty for our sins. We should gratefully and humbly accept with amazement that He did it for us—even for me—and repent and trust Him *now*, if we have not yet done so. If we have trusted Him, we need to share this life-changing and eternity-changing message of the cross with others and, by God's grace and strength, follow Jesus as our Lord every day.

FOUR KEY POINTS ABOUT THE CROSS AND RESURRECTION OF JESUS

A s a bridge between Part 1—'Were You There ... When They Crucified My Lord?' and Part 2—'Were You There When He Rose Up From The Grave?' we now look at four categories of reasons showing why you can safely believe in the resurrection of the Lord Jesus Christ.

But first, please read the Bible's summary of some of the appearances of the resurrected Lord Jesus Christ in 1 Corinthians 15:1–20.

One way only to be saved

The risen Jesus is the only Saviour and perfect God-Man.

The Bible says there is only one way to have our sins forgiven—one way to avoid Hell's eternal judgment and enjoy Heaven's blessing forever. Only through the risen Lord Jesus Christ can we receive eternal life now and never lose it.

When, with shame, we turn from our sins and trust Jesus Christ personally as our Lord and Saviour, we admit our failures and guilt, and turn our back on them. We thank Jesus for having borne those sins and their punishment in our place on the cross and for having risen again. We ask Him, the ever-living Saviour, to enter our life through the Holy Spirit. He does this to answer our heart-felt cry to Him in prayer. We individually ask Him to enter our sinful heart, cleanse it, and 'be merciful to me, a sinner.'

Jesus said: *'I am the way, the truth and the life: no one comes to the Father except through Me'* (John 14:6). The historic God-given message of Christianity about the Lord Jesus Christ is clear: *'There is no other name given under Heaven amongst men whereby we must be saved'* (Acts 4:12). Jesus is the only Saviour. No one else can forgive and save guilty people. 'Jesus' means 'God saves.' He is both fully God and perfect, sinless Man. He is 'Emmanuel—God with us.'

Two things Jesus did to save those who trust Him

Jesus died as a perfect sacrifice.
He rose from death and lives now.

Because Jesus was sinless, He never had to pay the penalty for His own sins. He had none to pay for. His thoughts, words, deeds and intentions were all entirely without fault and pleased God the Father—unlike you and me. Because He was eternally God, by dying on the cross He frees any sinner that comes to Him from sin and judgment *forever*. He gives eternal life now to all who believe in Him.

Because Jesus rose again from the dead on the third day, He defeated death and indwells anyone who asks Him into their life. The power of His resurrection life in the new Christian produces the great joy of becoming a 'new creation' in Christ, as 2 Corinthians 5:17 proclaims. Why? Because he has been 'born again' by God's Spirit, as Jesus promised in John 3:1–17.

But a vital result of Jesus' resurrection is that because God the Father raised Him from death, He thereby showed that He accepted Jesus' payment for my sins in full at Calvary's cross. I go free because He paid for me. As one hymn puts it:

Because the sinless Saviour died,
my sinful soul is counted free.
For God the just is satisfied
to look on Him and pardon me.

Three reasons why we are sure Jesus rose again
- The Bible says so.
- Overwhelming evidence.
- Changed lives.

But how can we be certain that all this is right? How can we know it is true?

First, because the Bible says so. The Bible is God's written word, written by fallible, but holy, men under the inspiration of the infallible third person of the Trinity, God the Holy Spirit. In context, there is no contradiction in the Bible. Jesus taught that was so, and so did the apostles. Every born-again person comes to know the infallible Author, God Himself, and begins to understand, read and love His infallible book, the Bible. We need no other authority to rely on. There is strong evidence to show that the Bible is God's infallible word—for example the fulfilled prophecies at the cross that we saw in Part 1—but we need no evidence when God speaks!

Second, there is also overwhelming evidence that Jesus died and rose again. Non-biblical writers and sources also evidence the fact of the resurrection. No properly constituted Court of Law would deny that there were far more credible, corroborating, and first-hand witnesses of good character to the resurrection than are needed to 'prove' anything in court today. Many of those early witnesses were so assured of the truth of the resurrection of Jesus from the grave that they suffered cruel persecution, imprisonment and even death rather than deny it.

And third, the changed lives of all who met the once crucified and now living Jesus demonstrated it was so. Some were always open-minded. Some, like Thomas, started as sceptical doubters. Others once cruelly opposed Christ. Think of the arch-persecutor, Saul, who was miraculously changed by the living Saviour. He became Paul, the Apostle, and wrote a large proportion of the New Testament as led by the Holy Spirit. Each changed person said the change was because they had met and yielded to Jesus after He rose again. They knew He had borne their wrongdoing and judgment, and rose to grant them eternal life now, and forever.

Four convincing pieces of evidence that Jesus rose

- Christ is unique.
- His resurrection was an accepted fact at the time it happened.
- Where was Jesus Christ's dead body?
- Lives are changed even today.

First, the Lord Jesus Christ is unique. There is no one like Jesus. He is not a religious leader among religious leaders: He is God in flesh amongst mere men. Expect the miraculous about and from Him. Did He provide the miraculous? Yes, He did! He was conceived by God the Holy Spirit through Mary, a virgin. His flawless, loving, holy and perfect life showed He was God in flesh. His teaching has never been surpassed by anyone or any religion anywhere. Even as a young boy in the temple He taught deep truth to experienced teachers of God's law. His amazing miracles acted as signs to show that He was God the Son, the ever-living Son of God, and one with the Father and the Holy Spirit. His death on the cross, as our substitute, sin-bearer, and Saviour—and the timing of that death—could only have been arranged by God's divine mind and hand. So, we should expect Jesus' miraculous resurrection from the dead and then an equally miraculous ascension to Heaven. One day He will, again miraculously, return to earth in great power and glory as 'King of Kings and Lord of Lords.'

Everything about Jesus was always miraculously different. He was, is, and always will be unique. But, amazingly, His birth, life, teaching, miracles, death, resurrection, and ascension were all foretold accurately in the Scriptures by direct prophecies and by providing other events that pictured those amazing truths about Jesus hundreds of years before He came. Prophecy said He would rise! He did!

Second, it was an accepted fact, with no counter argument at the time. When I wrote this part of this book, the UK Prime Minister, Boris Johnson, was in intensive care (ICU) with Covid-19. If I stated later that he had been a Covid-19 victim, no one argued about that well-known fact and common ground. It's the same about Jesus' resurrection. Those living when it happened never needed to prove it. Over 500 people saw Him at one time. People in large crowds, in groups, individually and in pairs met Him in various places and circumstances, and at different times. Everyone knew that many people had seen and met the risen Jesus after His well-attested death on the cross in crowded Jerusalem. When the apostles preached about Jesus, very soon after His death and resurrection, they never needed or tried to prove that He had died and risen. They did not need to. Everyone knew about it. It was a 'hot potato,' agreed by all.

Third, where was Jesus Christ's dead body? It was never produced. All that a person or faction needed to do to undermine the claim that Jesus rose again, was to provide the corpse. No one ever did. Neither were any remains found. And neither was anyone found alive who had previously claimed to have been Jesus. Where did Jesus go? There was never a trace of this high profiled person. Not a single witness came forward to say 'I saw the failed Jesus there,' or 'I found His body, remains or skeleton.' We know why! It is because Jesus rose from the grave and then ascended into Heaven.

Friend or foe, Christian or atheist or agnostic, religious or irreligious, all agree that Jesus, His death and His resurrection were very high profile. So was His body. It was battered, scourged and nailed to a cross, where a Roman spear finally pierced it. That body was moved from the cross to a tomb, by approval and oversight of the Governor, Pilate, and a senior Roman Centurion. All those who denied that Jesus rose had to do was to show where His body was. To destroy Christianity, they simply needed to disprove the resurrection by producing His dead body. The opposing Jewish religious leaders would have loved that, as the last nail in the coffin of resurrection! It would have ruined Christianity. The Romans, too, would have welcomed that, in order to crush another possible popular uprising in following another 'king.' The disciples' testimony would have died overnight. If Jesus stayed dead, why did no one produce the body? Those saying He did not die at all must explain why no one saw Him somewhere else, or revealed a cowering fraudster trying to hide from everyone? Why has no trace of the 'non-resurrected Jesus,' or of His corpse, skeleton, or human remains ever been produced? A fake resurrection could so easily have been exposed.

Fourth, millions of people throughout history, and today, insist that the risen Lord Jesus has changed them. They testify that when they trusted in the risen Saviour, who was punished for their sins on the cross, their lives were changed from the point in time when He came into their hearts. Some records of changed lives are in the Bible. Some are

historically well known. Some are little known. And there are millions today worldwide. And it is still going on across the world.

I just received an email from a once violent prisoner. He claimed a few years ago that he met the risen Jesus by faith. He turned from his sins to receive Jesus in his life as his living Lord and Saviour. First his cellmate, then his two grandparents, then his sister and mother came to rejoice in knowing Jesus living in them too! They were all convinced by how God changed his life since he received Christ. Think of Dr Barnardo, William Booth, William Wilberforce or Florence Nightingale. All were saved by Jesus and changed. Millions of others know that too. Do you?

Romans 10:9 says: *'if you confess with your mouth the Lord Jesus and believe in your heart that God has raised Him from the dead, you will be saved.'* That shows how to become 'born again.' It confirms 2 Corinthians 5:17: *'If anyone is in Christ, he is a new creation; old things have passed away; behold all things have become new.'* One of those changed people is sharing these words with you now! I love the rousing hymn and chorus, 'He lives!' The chorus of that hymn declares:

He lives! He lives!
Christ Jesus lives today.
He walks with me and talks with me
Along life's narrow way.
He lives! He lives!
Salvation to impart.
You ask me how I know He lives:
He lives within my heart!

The Lord Jesus Christ, who died and lives forever, is still the only Saviour from sin. He pardons, cleanses, changes, blesses and helps everyone who trusts in Him. That includes you. If you do not know Him yet, please come to Him now.

There is no shortage of objective and factual evidence that Jesus' resurrection is a historical fact. But the final piece of compelling evidence is that you can have your own your personal testimony to its truth if you receive Christ in your heart (John 1:12). If you do not repent of sin and receive Him, you can have no such testimony to give. If you do receive Him, eternal life and knowing the risen Jesus in your life begin and are a reality. And Heaven awaits you after this life!

One strong branch of evidence that you know the risen Lord and are yielded to Him is that others will see it in your life. Romans 14:9 says, *'For this reason Christ died and returned to life so that He might be the Lord of both the dead and the living.'* The 'dead' who know the risen Jesus have no problems. They are in Heaven now! The 'living'—which (hopefully!) includes you and me!—belong to Jesus because we repented of our sins and trusted Jesus as Lord and Saviour. Repentance from sins is the first step we take to make Jesus Christ our Lord. But it does not finish at conversion. It carries on day by day as we continue to turn from sin and selfish choices and move off the throne of our lives to bow before King Jesus. When we fail, we ask Him to forgive and cleanse us, and we yield to Him afresh. We now need to have an audience with this King of kings every day when we read our Bibles and have a quiet time of personal prayer. We are on duty for our King 24/7. We must honour Him in what we do, what we say, what we do not do, and what we do not say. We represent Him in this sinful word and work and pray to help other sinners bow to Him too, and in so doing have their sins forgiven and receive eternal life and a home in Heaven! Meanwhile we meet with others who know Him, in our churches and fellowship groups, for Bible study, prayer together, fellowship, friendship and for worship together on Sunday, the Lord's Day.

Part 2

WERE YOU THERE—WHEN HE ROSE UP FROM THE GRAVE?

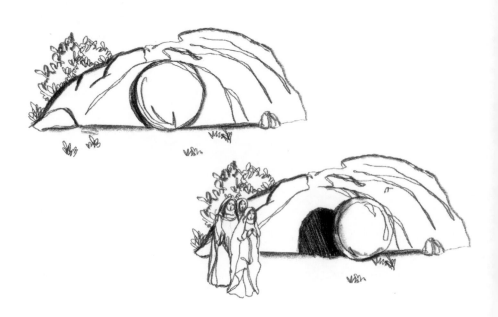

Setting the scene

1 CORINTHIANS 15:1–11
ALSO REFER TO: MATTHEW 28:1–47; MARK 15:40–47; 16:1–20[1]; LUKE 24:1–53;
JOHN 20:1–31; 21:1–25; ACTS 26:1–23

The Cross and Resurrection of Jesus 'of first importance'

A vital short statement in the New Testament defining the gospel (the 'good news') is 1 Corinthians 15:3–4. It sets the scene for Part 2 of this book on meeting first-hand witnesses who met Jesus Christ after He died on the cross and rose again. He died there bearing our sins and the punishment for them that we deserve. Christ's cross is literally 'crucial' to Christianity. The word 'crucial' comes from the Latin word 'crux' which means 'cross.' Collins English Dictionary defines 'crucial' as 'involving a final or supremely important decision or event.' When Jesus, fully God and fully Man, was nailed to that cruel cross as a sinless and perfect offering for us, the whole of God the Father's wrath on sin fell on His Son in my place. That is why I was forgiven, when I repented from my sins and put all my trust in Jesus. When He shed His blood on the cross it was the 'final event' of paying for guilty sinners' sins, as Jesus cried out in triumph *'It is finished'* ('completed' or 'accomplished.')

Along with Jesus' resurrection from the dead, His sacrifice on the cross was *the* 'supremely important event' of history. If Jesus had not died and risen again—which He did exactly as He often said that He would—there could be no forgiveness for *anyone*, no restoration to God, no eternal life, and no hope or certainty of spending eternity with God in Heaven. That is why the apostle Paul, who met the risen Jesus dramatically on the Damascus road, insisted in 1 Corinthians 15, that it is 'of first importance that Christ died for our sins according to the Scriptures, that he was buried, that he was raised on the third day according to the Scriptures.'

Make it crystal clear

That is why everyone who shares the good news with others must make it crystal clear both that Christ died for guilty sinners and rose again, and also why Jesus died and rose again. The crucial teaching of the cross and the resurrection must feature as the 'final [and] supremely important events.' Both are 'crucial.' To trust in Jesus is also the 'supremely important decision' to make in life. Whenever someone hears and understands that he is cut off from holy God because of his sin for which he will be punished, and that Jesus loves him and died in his place for him on the cross to take his penalty for all his sins of thought, word, deed, motive and omission, he has a 'crucial' decision to make. As God the Holy Spirit convicts him of his guilt and shows him his need to turn in repentant prayer to Christ, once crucified and now risen from the dead, he will realise that his decision to turn from sin and trust Jesus is, by far, the *most* 'supremely important decision or event' in his life, too.

If Jesus had stayed dead, the 'whole deal' of forgiveness would have been impossible! The resurrection without the cross could save no one. The cross without the resurrection would be a complete failure. If you are able, read Day One's *The Resurrection: The unopened gift*, it frankly and openly shows how the Christian message would have crumbled to nothing if Christ had stayed dead.

Consider the results that would have followed a 'failed' resurrection:

- Christ becomes incredible—He said He would rise again.
- Jesus' death on the cross becomes a calamity. God the Father showed He accepted Jesus' death on the cross for sinners by raising Him from the tomb. No rising from the dead would mean no acceptance.
- Jesus becomes either the deceiver or the deceived: not God the Son.
- Freedom from judgment for our sins becomes impossible: if Jesus died and did not rise, then He cannot be the eternal Judge. Thus, He can neither acquit us nor be qualified to successfully bear our

judgment on the cross. Neither can He judge sinners for their sins eternally. Of course, that encourages some to deny the resurrection of Jesus: they do not like to think they have to face the holy and eternal judge. They think that to accept the resurrection is rather like a turkey voting for Christmas!

- Death becomes dominant. By rising from death, Jesus conquered death. If he did not rise again, death conquered Him: He then becomes the big failure.
- Faith becomes futile. Why trust a failure at all, let alone for eternity?
- A failed and dead Christ cannot return in power, glory and triumph. So there is no second coming.
- There can be no Heaven to spend with a 'Saviour' who stays dead.
- Christianity becomes just one of many similar religions. The life, death and resurrection of Jesus, our 'Emmanuel—God with us', makes Christianity unique. *Religion tries to go up* to go to God and fails—*Jesus came down*, died, rose and ascended to Heaven and succeeds in getting us there. No religious leader ever could or did that! Only Jesus saves.
- Jesus cannot live in and change my heart now, as my living Saviour, as the Bible says He does if I am 'born again.' A dead Saviour cannot live in my heart or be received by faith.

So, it is vital to be sure that His resurrection did happen and was well witnessed. He did rise and His resurrection is well witnessed! In this book we meet people recorded in Scripture as meeting the risen Saviour: there were others, but here are good, reliable, first-hand, corroborated witnesses acceptable in any properly constituted Law Court, anywhere.

You can read about the people who met the risen Lord Jesus Christ in the New Testament passages already mentioned.

Here are the people we will meet:

- In 1 Corinthians 15: Peter, the disciples (several times), 500 people at one time, James, all the Apostles and Saul (who became Paul) on the Damascus Road.

- In Matthew 28: Mary Magdalene, the 'other Mary,' other women who were there, and the eleven disciples.
- In Mark 15–16: Mary Magdalene, Mary (James' mother), Salome, the two travellers in the country and the eleven disciples again.
- In Luke 24: the same women with the spices (including Joanna and other unnamed women), the two Emmaus Road disciples, Simon, and the disciples without 'doubting' Thomas.
- In John 20–21: Mary Magdalene, the disciples first without Thomas, then with Thomas, then the disciples often, and the breakfast on the beach with some of the fishermen disciples— including Simon Peter, Thomas, Nathanael, and two others.
- In Acts 26: Saul who became Paul.

As with most events in New Testament times, the four Gospel writers rarely write identical accounts, but what they say is never contradictory, when it is read in context. Like reporters at a football match who all cover the goals scored, these writers all cover the major issue—Jesus Christ died and is risen! At different places, in different circumstances, with varying numbers of people, for varying periods of time, these witnesses give good, corroborated evidence that the One who died to save us, now lives to be our Saviour and to give us eternal life. We will begin to meet them in the next chapter.

Please read 1 Corinthians 1:1–11 now and then work your way through the accounts in Matthew, Mark, Luke and John. As you do, ask yourself, 'Did Christ die for me?' and 'Do I know He is living in me as my Lord and Saviour?'

NOTES

1 See the footnote on page 169 of Day One book *Mark Time*, chapter 52 re Mark 16:9–20. Briefly, some versions of the Bible omit these verses, some mark them as optional. The

reason they give is that the oldest manuscripts of Mark's gospel do not include them. They are, however, found in most reliable manuscripts and the early church fathers quoted them in letters that predate the earliest known manuscripts. Which manuscript did they get them from? Evidently, an older one they had but we do not. I regard these verses as God's word and what they teach is also fully consistent with the rest of the Bible.

The women

MATTHEW 28:1–10
ALSO REFER TO: MARK 16:1–11; LUKE 24:1–12; JOHN 20:1–2, 10–18

'A woman is the man for the job!'

I mentioned before that a Christian world mission organisation used to challenge Christian men by saying 'a woman is the man for the job!' Far more women than men were volunteering to go to live and work on overseas mission fields, to share the gospel of forgiveness through faith in Jesus Christ. Today it seems that Christian women are usually more willing than their male counterparts to sacrifice their comforts, personal hopes, ambitions, time and finance. Where are the committed Christian men who will lead by example in their own lives, their marriages and family lives, their churches and fellowships, and in missions to make Christ known at home and abroad?

Few male disciples were there

Few male disciples were present as Jesus died on that cross to take the punishment for our sin, but the women were there. Women were also the first at the empty tomb after Jesus miraculously rose from the dead. Later the apostles *'joined together constantly in prayer' along with the women and Mary the mother of Jesus, and with His brothers'* (Acts 1:14).

A vital role

These committed women were at the cross, at the empty tomb, and at Pentecost. They witnessed the blood of Jesus being shed when He was judged for our sins. They met the living Jesus, risen from the dead. They saw the Holy Spirit's coming on the crowd which listened to Peter as he proclaimed his crucified and risen Lord. *'About three thousand'* people were saved and added to the fledgling church (Acts 2:41). These women were godly and faithful disciples with a great role to play. Today, women who live for Christ still play a vital role. But who are these women in the four Gospel accounts?

Put the Gospel records together

Matthew, Mark, Luke and John do not try to cover all the names of all the women who accompany Mary Magdalene, Mary the mother of James, Salome, and Joanna. John only focuses on Mary Magdalene. He does not comment on the names or number of other women. All four Gospel writers mention Mary Magdalene. She is the first person whom Scripture records as meeting her resurrected Lord Jesus. Assuming the 'other Mary' mentioned by Matthew is Mary the mother of James, she is named three times. Mark names Salome, and Luke names Joanna. Luke is known for his detailed writing. (If you read the Acts of the Apostles you will notice that.) He reminds us that there are 'others with them.' These women witness not just one, but two, gleaming angels (as in John's Gospel). They bow down to them in fright. The angels confirm Jesus is 'living' and remind them of Jesus' words that He would be *delivered into the hands of sinful men, be crucified and the third day be raised again.* They then remember Jesus' telling them the same thing before He died and rose again. Together they all tell *this to the apostles,* (called the 'eleven' since Judas' death.) But the eleven do not believe the women, so Peter wisely goes himself to investigate, as we will see in the next chapter. Luke 23:55–56 confirms that these women, *who had come with Jesus from Galilee,* followed Joseph of Arimathea to the tomb on the Friday. They then *saw the tomb and how His body was laid in it.* They need to do that to bring the spices to treat the body after the Sabbath. Their evidence is rock solid that Jesus died and that His tomb is empty on that third day. They also record that the angels confirmed that Jesus 'is risen.' Remember that Jesus, clearly and often, predicted exactly that this would happen. He *never* got or gets things wrong.

No Gospel writer contradicts another, but sometimes one will emphasise aspects separately from the others. In a court of law that would add to the credibility of evidence—if their accounts had been artificially 'cobbled' together, they would make sure that every piece of so-called 'evidence' fitted in exactly with the others. Nothing is more obvious to the trained lawyer than doctored 'identical evidence.' Legitimate variations have the ring of reality about them, for instance:

Matthew reports that Mary Magdalene and *'the other Mary,'* (James' mother, no doubt) see the empty tomb and, like Mark, witness one angel there. Angels can come unnoticed (Hebrews 13:2). They can come and go in a flash, either seen or unseen, so perhaps the second angel came later? Or perhaps they were so overawed by the 'lead angel' that the women did not notice his companion. We do not know or need to know. They then go and tell the disciples as instructed by the angel. After they set off to see the disciples, Jesus comes to them suddenly and greets them. They grasp His feet in worship. He tells them not to be afraid but to go to tell his brothers to go to Galilee where He will meet them. Is that His physical brothers, or His spiritual brothers, or both?

Mark confirms much of what Matthew says. But he adds that their first reaction, in fear, is to want to run away and tell no one. After that,

Mary Magdalene does go as told by the angel, to tell the disciples. Perhaps Matthew records that Jesus tells her not to be afraid because she is so frightened initially!

John describes Mary standing outside the empty tomb, after returning from telling Peter about it, and after he has visited the empty tomb with John ('the one Jesus loved'). They both see the empty tomb and the folded graveclothes of Jesus—but no angels. (Remember they can come and go, seen or unseen.) They return to their homes. Mary is then crying outside the tomb. She then sees two angels in white. They are sitting where Jesus' body had been. After having a conversation with them, she sees someone she thinks is the gardener. But when the 'gardener' calls her by name, she then knows it is Jesus. He tells her not to hold Him physically. He wants her faith to be real and spiritual not just 'touchy feely.' She then goes back to the disciples and openly tells them, 'I have seen the Lord!'

All these accounts blend and fit together. What can we learn from them?

- The key facts of the gospel are the life, death, resurrection and ascension of Jesus, and God's giving His Holy Spirit to each convert and so to all the church. Always remember those vital verses which we looked at in Chapter 1 of Part 1 of this book. Nothing means or matters more than Jesus dying on the cross as our sin-bearer and substitute to take the punishment we deserve. We would remain under eternal death-sentence in Hell if Christ had not died for our sins. As vital as that is, the twin truth that He is risen again from the dead, enables Him now to become the indwelling living Lord of all who receive Him by faith. Jesus does all this by the Holy Spirit. Our salvation is triply endorsed, by God the Father, the Son, and the Holy Spirit.
- The death and resurrection of Jesus are both factual and well evidenced. By 'well evidenced', I mean that the evidence is excellent both in the calibre and the number of its witnesses. Any

advocate in court would delight to call witnesses like this to support the case he has to make.

- If you have received Christ as your Saviour, you have both a duty and a privilege to share with others how they can and need to turn from their sin and surrender their lives to the Lord Jesus Christ as their Lord and Saviour.

- Pray daily for those you get to know, that they will be blessed by the Lord. Remember that the best argument that we have a risen Saviour living within is the amazing change He makes in the lives of those who receive Him. In short, conversion to Jesus works! We should seek, by God's grace and help, to live out the reality of the gospel by holy living, godly thinking, right words, honest witness and relying on the Lord to keep us, help us and use us.

- Remember to thank, praise and honour your unique and sinlessly perfect Saviour, Lord and God. Worship, trust and obey Him!

Peter

1 CORINTHIANS 15:3–8
ALSO REFER TO: MATTHEW 28:5–7, 9–10; MARK 16:1–2; LUKE 24:9–12, 34; JOHN
10:1–9, 19–31; 21:1–24

Call him 'Peter,' 'Simon Peter,' 'Simon,' or 'Cephas'

Peter is the most colourful of all the Lord's disciples. He is mostly called *'Peter'* ('a stone'), but often called *'Simon'* ('hearing') or *'Simon Peter.'* A few times *'Cephas'* ('a rock') is used, unless *'Cephas'* is translated *'Peter.'* We simply call him *'Peter.'*

Different from the others?

All about Peter seems a little 'different.' He is the one to identify Jesus as 'the Christ, the Son of the living God.' Jesus says that this had been divinely revealed to him. Then soon after that, Peter tells Jesus that it is not true that Jesus will suffer, die and be raised from the dead. This was despite the fact that Jesus told His disciples that He would suffer in those ways and rise again! Jesus warns Peter that Satan is deceiving him by that error. We need, as a point of principle, trust in obedience, to always accept what God says to us. That will always be in concert with the Bible as the true and only word of God. Never doubt the Bible!

Peter is the first disciple to promise rashly to Jesus that he will follow Him, even if no one else does. (All the disciples then say the same thing.) He alone resists violently at Jesus' arrest in the Garden of Gethsemane, and cuts off the ear of Malchus, the High Priest's servant, with a sword. (At this worst time in Jesus' earthly life, He promptly and graciously heals it.) Soon before Jesus is crucified, with pressure mounting on Peter, he denies that he knows or follows Jesus three times. He then goes out and weeps 'bitterly' as a result of his denials. Peter's sad experience reminds us how easy it is to make generous and extensive promises to

Chapter 3

God in a time of conscious blessing, or in the heat of the moment, or because of well-meant pressure from others, and then regret later what you promised. Instant obedience is necessary, but some things need to be prayed over and thought out rather than to promise rashly as Peter did. We need to keep close to Jesus in our personal devotions each day. Then we will act less rashly and with greater spiritual understanding.

"God has raised this Jesus to life"

Peter after the death and resurrection of Jesus

But we now will look at Peter *after* our Lord and Saviour, Jesus, died and rose again. Sadly, all the disciples feel defeated, guilty and try to hide from public view. They cower in fear, knowing that their Lord has been cruelly and wickedly treated and crucified. Strangely, not one of them remembers that Jesus often said that this would happen. Peter is normally the most headstrong and impetuous of them by far. But now he is simply just one of the disillusioned, miserable, crumbling failures that the disciples have become. There seems to be no hope, no good news, no way out—and the opposition is so very strong.

Who goes counter-flow when told that Jesus is alive?

1 Corinthians 15:5 tells us that the once crucified, now risen Lord Jesus Christ, appears to Peter, and then to the twelve. Significantly, Peter is the first person who Paul records as having met the risen Lord. But this is after Mary Magdalene and the women with her have seen the once occupied and guarded tomb of Jesus. It is now empty and open for all to see or inspect. They see angels, but more important still, they later meet the risen Jesus Himself. Mary Magdalene talks with Him. First, the angel, and then the Lord Jesus, tell the women to go to inform the disciples that

Jesus is risen and will meet them in Galilee. The women go, as instructed, and tell the disciples. The disciples' first reaction is sheer unbelief. But one of them goes counter-flow to the rest. Can you guess who that is?

Who else but Peter?

Who else but Peter? He is not convinced yet that Jesus is alive but goes to inspect the site for himself. He is accompanied by John, who outruns him to get there first, but then hangs back. Peter enters the tomb and sees it all for himself, including Jesus' graveclothes through which His resurrected body has passed. Peter returns home, wondering about what he saw. *En route,* Jesus appears personally to a bewildered Peter, perhaps in the same way that He earlier appeared to Mary Magdalene.

Confirmation from others

Luke 24:34 confirms 1 Corinthians 15:5 that Peter meets Jesus before the other disciples do. The two travellers on the road to Emmaus go straight to 'the eleven' [the disciples] to tell them that they met the resurrected Christ. They meet *'the eleven and those with them assembled together.'* *'Those with them'* are Mary Magdalene's friends who are also there to tell those sceptical disciples the same thing! On hearing that the two Emmaus travellers have met their risen Lord, those women respond, *'It is true! The Lord has risen and has appeared to Simon.'* But the other disciples have not yet met the living Jesus themselves. God is

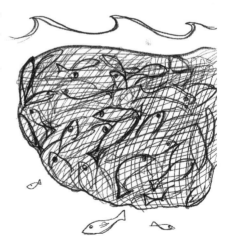

preparing them for that. He *always* prepares people's minds before they trust in Jesus. (Maybe He is preparing your mind now?) In the interest of accuracy, it should be said that Peter is not *named individually* in the accounts of those disciples who do later meet the resurrected Jesus in Matthew 28:8; Mark 16:7 and John 20:19–31, but he is clearly one of the disciples and is with them, as Matthew 28:8 strongly implies, and as the angel at the tomb knows and states specifically in Mark 16:7. John 20:19–31 says *'the disciples were together with the doors locked for fear of the Jews.'* They were there as a body. Verse 24 calls the *assembly* of them *'the twelve'* (although Judas was dead). It specifically says that Thomas was noted as not being there *'with the disciples'* for the first time Jesus appeared to Thomas, but that *'Thomas was with them'* a week later when Jesus appeared *'in the house again.'* Surely high-profile Peter is counted in the *'disciples'* and *'the twelve,'* especially when absentees, like Thomas at the first appearance, would be mentioned.

Peter sees Jesus again, when with the disciples

So, when Jesus appears to the disciples soon after, we can safely assume that Peter is there. He sees Thomas come to faith in Christ. The previous arch-doubter's words *'My Lord and my God'* show he now believes that Christ was nailed to the cross to bear his sins and their penalty. He now trusts in his heart in the Lord Jesus Christ, who conquered death and lives forever. By the Holy Spirit, Jesus now lives in Thomas' heart—and in the heart of everyone today who turns from sin and receives Christ by faith. Do you believe in Jesus like that? Are you saved by faith in Christ alone? (John 20:19–28).

Three times three is restoration!

Peter earlier denied Jesus *three times* before Jesus was crucified. Now, the risen Lord appears on the beach to Peter and the six other disciples who go fishing with him. While they are fishing, Jesus appears on the beach and cooks them breakfast. They do not then know that He comes to restore Peter. When Peter sees Jesus on the shore, he jumps overboard to get to Him. He is serious now about knowing and following Jesus, despite feeling so wretched at having let Him down. Again, *three times* Jesus asks Peter directly if he loves Him as His Lord and Saviour. (Jesus' word for love means 'love with full commitment.') *Three times* Peter effectively answers 'Yes.' But he uses a lesser word for love than the word Jesus uses. The failed disciple is still aware of his sins and does not want to rush in rashly again as he did before. Jesus graciously accepts that and tells Peter three times (another three!) to feed and take care of His sheep. The Good Shepherd, Jesus, who gave His life for His sheep, refers to guilty and lost people who have trusted Him and joined His flock, the worldwide church, as 'sheep.' You can be included! If you know Him as your Shepherd-Saviour, you can be absolutely sure of having eternal life now and being in Heaven with Him forever (see, John 10:27–30).

Jesus shows that Peter's repentance and commitment to Christ is accepted, and the restored disciple and Apostle comes back as an under-shepherd of the flock of his Chief and Good Shepherd, the Lord Jesus Christ. When God saves you, He cleanses you from sin, changes you and uses you. Those who have failed and have been restored by God's amazing grace are in a good position to help other strugglers and failures! Peter will do that.

Jesus discusses other things with Peter, including that Peter will one day face death for being His devoted disciple. Peter the sad failure, is now Peter the restored servant! God will use him mightily in the days ahead, including soon preaching the gospel with God's power on the Day of Pentecost, when about 3,000 people trust Jesus and are saved.

Again, may I ask you; do *you* trust in Jesus? Are *you* saved? He is only ever a simple sincere prayer away from you.

The two travellers

LUKE 24:13–35; MARK 16:12–13

Good witnesses

We have been getting to know 'the people who met the risen Lord.' The death of Jesus, to bear our sins and God the Father's penalty of judgment against them, and the rising of Jesus from the tomb on the third day, are very well evidenced by plenty of known, credible, reliable, first-hand eye (and ear!) witnesses. Their testimonies corroborate each other. In any properly constituted court of law, that is very strong evidence. Add to that the fact that Jesus both claimed and showed Himself to be God in flesh. (As one little girl described Jesus to her mum, 'Jesus is God with skin on.') Then consider that Jesus predicted perfectly accurately, on numerous occasions, exactly what would happen to Him. You can then begin to understand why one High Court Judge stated that there was more evidence for the resurrection of Jesus from the dead than for any other event in ancient history.

Minds disengaged?

Yet the disciples seemed to disengage their minds and their memories of Jesus' words, predictions and miracles. They are so upset and feel so defeated that their emotions overcome both their faith and their logic. We all can be a bit like that in a crisis. How important it is for us each day to read, understand, know, believe, learn and apply God's word to our daily lives. We reap the benefit of so doing in the 'down times' of our lives.

'They think it's all over'

Here are two travellers on the way to Emmaus. They knew Jesus before He died on the cross. They are convinced that He was at least 'a prophet, powerful in word and deed before God and all the people.' Remembering who Jesus was, and what He said and did, they 'had hoped that He *was* the one who *was going to* redeem Israel.' They even had heard the women's testimony about the empty tomb and knew that Peter and John had been there, which confirmed their testimony. (It seems they have not yet heard that Jesus appeared to Mary Magdalene and her friends, or later to Peter.) But now every hope has gone. Unbelief reigns. The Scriptures are ignored. Jesus' words and promises are forgotten. That is why all they once felt confident and happy about concerning Jesus, and following Him, is now spoken of as being in the past and so not true anymore: hence their sad words '*had* hoped,' and saying that Jesus '*was*' the one who '*was going*' to redeem Israel, rather than '*is* the one who will redeem Israel.' As one football commentator famously put it, 'They think it's all over.'

The unknown stranger

As they discuss these sad thoughts, in their seven-mile-long walk to Emmaus from Jerusalem, an unrecognised man comes up to them and walks with them. We know who the 'stranger' is because the Bible tells us: but they have no idea yet. If angels can make themselves unrecognisable, the Lord of the angels certainly can! With 'downcast' faces, they answer His question, 'What are you discussing together?' and then talk dejectedly about their sadness and their huge disappointment about 'Jesus of Nazareth.' The unknown stranger, the risen Lord Jesus Christ, is extremely frank with them: 'How foolish you are, and how slow of heart to believe all that the prophets have spoken! Did not the Christ have to suffer these things and then enter His glory?' He then explains from all the Old Testament (then called the 'law and the prophets' or, as here, 'Moses and all the prophets') what 'all the Scriptures' say about the Lord Jesus Christ. Jesus believes the whole of the word of God and applies it all to Himself, the only sinless and perfect

Man, the unique eternal Son of God, the Son of Man, and God the Son. He is one Person in the Trinity with God the Father and God the Holy Spirit. Jesus teaches them a lesson seven miles long from the Old Testament. He obviously regards and respects it as God's word. So should we: the Old and the New Testaments together form God's complete and infallible written word.

Breaking bread—open eyes, Scriptures, hearts and understanding

A little later they invite Him to dine with them. They urge Him to stay with them, which He does. Today, Jesus still dwells with and in all who invite Him! At the table, they recognise Him as Jesus when He takes the bread, breaks it, and gives thanks. Their eyes are opened—no doubt they think back to that time when Jesus said that His body would be broken on the cross, when He would die there as our sin-bearer and substitute. Then Jesus disappears as quickly as he had appeared. Their hearts had burned within them as He opened up the Scriptures to them. That is still the way that He speaks to us today, aided by His Holy Spirit. Their eyes, their hearts, their understanding, and God's word have all been opened by Jesus. That is how God saves people today. He deals with our hearts through His word as the Holy Spirit makes it real to us.

Open mouths too!

But now their mouths are opened too! They go to tell

the disciples that the resurrected Jesus has met and taught them. Those once sceptical disciples have just heard from the women who also met the risen Lord. They also have heard that Jesus has appeared to Peter. Here is layer upon layer of good evidence coming from many sources! That is usually how God convinces sinners to trust Him: He keeps on revealing truth to them until they repent and trust Him. If you are seeking God, keep reading His word, the Bible, always with the prayer that God will speak to you through it.

Soon the disciples will meet Jesus too. We will look at that in the next chapter. But we can learn a lot from these two travellers:

- Be honest with God about how you think and feel.
- Never think you are alone. Others believe in Him too!
- When God starts to speak to you through His word, keep listening.
- Weigh up the evidence but do not expect to see it all before you come to trust and follow Jesus. You have enough evidence already anyhow!
- Trust in the Lord Jesus Christ, His death and resurrection for you, and believe the Bible with all your heart and mind.
- Tell others about Jesus too: seek to be a blessing to them. This includes helping people to come to trust Christ and supporting fellow believers.

Chapter 5

The disciples

1 CORINTHIANS 15:1 –1 2
ALSO REFER TO: MATTHEW 28:1–20; MARK 16:1–20; LUKE 24:1–53;
JOHN 20:1–31; 21:1–14

The disciples as a group

We are 'meeting' people who met the Lord Jesus Christ after He had died on the cross. It was there that He bore our sins and God the Father's punishment on them, and then rose again from the dead on the third day from the new tomb of Joseph of Arimathea. So far, having set the scene, we have looked at some who met the risen Jesus. They are the women, Peter ('Simon Peter'), and two sad travellers on the seven-mile road between Jerusalem and Emmaus. Now we look at Jesus' disciples as a group. The Bible readings which cover this are as shown above. We will follow them in that order.

The 'Twelve' are sometimes known as the 'Eleven'—after Judas' death

Our resurrected Lord met individual disciples on various occasions: whether solo, in twos, in small groups, or as part of a big crowd. We now concentrate on the group of disciples known as the 'Twelve.' They are sometimes called the 'Eleven,' after Judas Iscariot committed suicide. But sometimes the same group is still called by their original title, the 'Twelve'. A 'disciple' is someone under another's teaching and discipline. He is committed to follow that person. The apostles were Jesus' special disciples: men who led the group with God-given authority to lead other disciples and churches. Their qualifications include the fact that they have met the Lord Jesus Christ after His resurrection.

God's word

God uses them and other leading spiritual disciples, under their influence and in close contact with them, to write the word of God in the New Testament. For that, they are infallibly inspired and guided to do so by the Holy Spirit, despite showing their own styles in their writings. God's holy and inspired word consists of sixty-six books: thirty-nine are in the Old Testament, and twenty-seven in the New Testament. The Old and New Testaments together form the entire, infallible and complete written word of God. Take nothing from it and add nothing to it. It is there daily to be read, learned, followed in Christian living, and taught and explained to Christians and non-Christians. Its central character is God the Son, the Lord Jesus Christ. That is how the Trinity of God the Father, God the Son, and God the Holy Spirit want it to be! God is One, and the three Persons of the Trinity are always in full accord and agreement! But the point right now is that the Spirit's inspiration and enabling, in producing the New Testament, comes through the apostles and through other leading disciples who worked closely with them, and are helped and influenced by, those apostles.

Risen Jesus in 1 Corinthians 15

Jesus, risen from the grave, appears to the disciples as a group. Here are two occasions, recorded by Paul, in 1 Corinthians 15:3 and 8:3:

For what I received I passed on to you as of first importance: that Christ died for our sins according to the Scriptures, 4 that he was buried, that he was raised on the third day according to the Scriptures, 5 and that he appeared to Peter, and then to the Twelve. 6 After that, he appeared to more than five hundred of the brothers at the same time, most of whom are still living, though some have fallen asleep. 7 Then he appeared to James, then to all the apostles, 8 and last of all he appeared to me also, as to one abnormally born.

Chapter 5

Variety of appearances

The first appearance of Jesus 'to the Twelve' is after He first meets Peter (when, as explained earlier, they are called the 'Eleven') in Luke 23:33–34. The second time is to 'all the apostles' after Jesus has appeared to the crowd of 500 brothers in Christ, and then separately to James. It seems that this is soon before the risen Jesus ascends to Heaven (Luke 24:50). An important point is the variety of appearances that Jesus makes. He shows Himself to some people once or twice and others more often, and also to vastly different numbers of people, in different circumstances, and at different times. This must be remembered when sceptical but non-sensical suggestions are made that the people who think they see Him are merely deluded or hallucinating. That is impossible with such differing people and varied circumstances. The same delusion never comes to so many different people in different circumstances. Nor will they all get over the 'delusion' at exactly the same time! All appearances cease after the time that Jesus ascends to Heaven! (Paul's case was different. As we shall see later in this book, the post-resurrection and post-ascension Christ appears to him from Heaven to speak to 'unconverted Saul' and meet him on the Damascus Road (Acts 26:12–18). He later becomes 'converted Paul!' He is always very sure that the resurrection of Christ is a solid fact!

Matthew 28:16–17 sees the risen Jesus appear to the Eleven on the mountain in Galilee. (The women had been told to tell them He would meet them there—and He did!) Some worshipped Him 'but some doubted.' This is so true of sinful human nature. The fact that even doubters ended up believing in Christ crucified and risen from the dead is a strong evidence for the reality of the historical resurrection.

Jesus then:

- Reminds them of His authority (as God the Son and the eternal Son of God).

- Commissions them to go and share the gospel message worldwide and make disciples out of their hearers everywhere.
- Confirms this is to be done 'in the name of the Father and of the Son and of the Holy Spirit' (note: three Persons but only one name because God is One).
- Teaches them to teach those who become Christians, by faith alone in Christ alone, to obey Him.
- Promises 'surely I am with you always, to the very end of the age' (Matthew 24:18–20).

It is not clear whether Mark 16:14–18 refers to the same actions as Matthew 24:18–20, or whether it is a similar event. It seems that at very least they slot in together. In Mark 16, Jesus appears to the Eleven as they eat together. He rebukes them for their unbelief in His resurrection. He then commissions them (in different words from Matthew 28) also to preach the gospel to everyone all over the world, and then encourages them by telling them the kind of things that will happen under God's hand to help them. His ascension happens later. After that they go out and preach 'everywhere.'

Luke 24:33–52: when the two on the Emmaus Road go to tell the disciples they have met the risen Jesus, rather like the women have done earlier after they see the risen Christ, they are first greeted by the news that 'the Lord has appeared to Peter!' They tell the disciples of their experience of Christ making Himself known in the breaking of bread. As they do, Jesus Himself is suddenly 'in the midst' of them all. That is proof upon proof upon proof that Jesus is alive from the dead. But they are scared, and Jesus comforts them, refers them to His crucifixion wounds, and uses logic to say that spirits do not have flesh and bones as He has.

Ample proof

The risen Christ, having fulfilled His own prophecies and given ample proof of His resurrection, now uses truth-based logic to convince them.

That is a good pattern for Christians to remember when speaking to others about Christ. Scripture first, facts next, and logical argument based on all of that—all pointing to the Lord Jesus Christ who died to be punished for our sins and rose again to be our living Lord now and in Heaven. Jesus then demonstrates He is more than a spirit, but is in His resurrection body, when He eats some fish! He then tells them to believe all the word of God, as then presented in the Old Testament, and opens the Scriptures to their understanding. That also happens when a sinner turns to Christ today! When we come to know the Author of the Bible, we begin to understand His book with the help of the Holy Spirit. Jesus then commissions them to share the gospel of repentance from sins, and their remission (which means complete forgiveness) starting near them in Jerusalem and then to 'all nations.' That is why He died and rose again— to see people saved from all over the world. That is why committed Christians show real interest in missions worldwide, by informing themselves of the position, praying often, and giving financially to support them. They want people all over the world to hear about the Lord Jesus Christ and put their trust in Him.

Witnesses to others to be saved

Once saved, we are to be His witnesses to others to be saved. Does that include you yet? Has Jesus saved you, yet? He then promises them that the Holy Spirit will come upon them to empower them to live for Him. When God commands Christians to do something in His word, He also empowers them. God's command is also His enabling. Later Jesus ascends to Heaven after blessing them. They then go to the temple to praise and bless God. What a transformation Jesus makes in our lives when we trust Him!

Jesus appears three times

John 20:19–31; 20:1–14: here we see Jesus appear three times, but we are also told, in John 20:30, that 'Jesus did many other miracles in the presence of His disciples, which are not recorded in this book.' The Bible is God's complete word with everything in it that we need to know about being saved and about Jesus, but it does not include all the details of His heavenly or earthly life, of course. It would take a huge library to even begin to record all that (see also, John 21:25).

First and second appearances are without, and then with, Thomas

The first two appearances to the disciples are, first, without Thomas and then with him. We will consider Thomas later in this book. Suffice it to say that, after not believing in Christ, he became convinced and then lived for Christ—a good example for all doubters who then come to faith in Jesus! It seems that the second appearance is probably the one, described above, in Luke's Gospel. As we have thought before, the Gospel writers record different aspects of the same situation, without contradicting each other, just as sports writers do when they describe a match. They all record the same result! In these two cases it is all to do with putting your faith in the Lord Jesus Christ who died on the cross for you and rose again. That gives us acceptance with God, eternal life, peace, a commission to tell others about Christ, and the Holy Spirit in our lives. We also learn that to believe the words of God, here through the Lord Jesus Christ, is far more important than living by sight alone. It is, by God's grace, faith in Jesus alone that saves us and so gives us eternal life. Nothing else can (Ephesians 2:8–9).

Third appearance of Jesus and Peter's restoration

The third appearance focuses on Peter's restoration to Jesus after his earlier sad three-part denial of Jesus. Perhaps you remember that Jesus asked him three times before his restoration, 'Do you love Me?' That is a question we should let Jesus ask us, remembering that love for Jesus is far more than just a gooey feeling. Jesus said in John 14:15, 'If you love Me keep my commandments' (NKJV, followed by ESV—NIV similarly says, 'If you love Me, you will obey what I command.') That includes all His commands made or confirmed as God the Son, including the timeless Ten Commandments. To love Christ will mean my life changes—not just my emotions. Nothing shows we love Jesus more than obeying Him.

Jesus' third appearance is while some of the disciples go fishing. They are Peter, Thomas, Nathanael, James and John, and two other unnamed disciples (of which one was probably John, who records the meeting.) They toil all night but catch nothing. In the morning they see a 'Stranger' on the beach (whom they do not recognise as Jesus, at first). He tells them to put the net over on the other side. They do and have such a huge catch of 153 fish that they cannot haul in the net. Peter jumps in the water to rush to Jesus, while the others tow in the net. Jesus is cooking breakfast for them and tells them to get some fish. Peter goes back to drag it in and have breakfast with Him. Strangely they dare not ask Him who He is, but they know! Almost as a footnote we learn that the net is not torn, despite the huge sudden catch! Then we read that moving conversation between Jesus and Peter, which leads to his restoration and reinstatement as an Apostle. God will greatly use him in the future, starting with his stirring gospel message on the Day of Pentecost.

There is much to learn from all these recorded samples of Jesus' meeting the disciples after He rose from the dead. Perhaps the main lesson is that God loves all who trust and follow Him even after failure. He always wants us to come back to Him. We must trust, worship, follow, serve, and tell others about Him—but, above all, love Him and keep close to Him in daily Bible reading, prayer, and meet with others in weekly fellowship each Lord's day and in Bible studies.

'Not wanting anyone to perish'

And, of course, we constantly see that Christ crucified and now risen from the grave still longs to see sinners repent and trust Him as their Saviour. That never changes. In His earthly ministry, Jesus told the inhabitants of Jerusalem, 'How often I have longed to gather your children together, as a hen gathers her chicks under her wings, but you were not willing!' (Luke 13:34; Matthew 23:37). 2 Peter 3:9 reminds us today that, 'The Lord is not slow in keeping his promise, as some understand slowness. He is patient with you, not wanting anyone to perish, but everyone to come to repentance.' If you have not responded to Him yet, why not do so now?

James, the brother of Jesus

GALATIANS 1:18–19; 2:9, 12; ACTS 12:17; 15:12–22; 21:18

Look for the right 'James'

The '*James*' we are considering now is named six times in the New Testament. The few verses quoted above have the name '*James*' italicised below for ease of reference. Those brief verses speak for themselves.

In the longer passage, Acts 12:12–22, see his name once, but notice that *James* takes the initiative in verse 13 as President of the Council, in a very detailed and crucial matter which involves many Christians and Christian leaders. He announces his decision in verse 19. He is in charge, under God.

- *Galatians 1:18–19*: 'Then after three years, I went up to Jerusalem to get acquainted with Peter and stayed with him fifteen days. I saw none of the other apostles—only *James*, the Lord's brother.'
- *Galatians 2:9*: '*James*, Peter and John, those reputed to be pillars, gave me and Barnabas the right hand of fellowship.'
- *Galatians 2:12*: 'Before certain men came from *James*.'
- *Acts 12:17*: 'Peter motioned with his hand for them to be quiet and described how the Lord had brought him out of prison. "Tell *James* and the brothers about this."'
- *Acts 15: 12–22*: 'Then all the multitude kept silent and listened to Barnabas and Paul declaring how many miracles and wonders God had worked through them among the Gentiles. 13 And after they had become silent, *James* answered, saying, "Men and brethren, listen to me: 14 "Simon has declared how God at the first visited the Gentiles to take out of them a people for His name. 15 "And with this the words of the prophets agree, just as it is written: 16 'After this I will return And will rebuild the tabernacle of David, which has fallen down; I will rebuild its

ruins, And I will set it up; 17 So that the rest of mankind may seek the LORD, Even all the Gentiles who are called by My name, Says the LORD who does all these things.' 18 "Known to God from eternity are all His works. 19 "Therefore I judge that we should not trouble those from among the Gentiles who are turning to God, 20 "but that we write to them to abstain from things polluted by idols, from sexual immorality, from things strangled, and from blood. 21 "For Moses has had throughout many generations those who preach him in every city, being read in the synagogues every Sabbath." 22 Then it pleased the apostles and elders, with the whole church, to send chosen men of their own company to Antioch with Paul and Barnabas, namely, Judas who was also named Barsabbas, and Silas, leading men among the brethren.'

• Acts 21:18: 'The next day Paul and the rest of us went to see James, and all the elders were present.'

Crucified, punished, dead—and rose again!

We continue to 'meet' people who met the risen Lord Jesus Christ, God the Son. He died on the cross to bear our sins. Jesus was punished in our place in darkness divinely sent at mid-day. He willingly suffered there out of sight from the gathered crowd, as in anguish He paid, in three divinely concentrated hours, the eternal penalty for our sins from God the Father. On the third day He rose from the grave. The tomb was empty! We have seen already that the once crucified, but now risen, loving Lord met the women who came there, then Simon Peter, then the two travellers to Emmaus, and then the gathered disciples.

Which James?

But we are also told that, between appearing to the crowd of *'five hundred of the brothers,'* which we will look at in the next chapter, and the apostles, whom we included when considering the disciples, He *'Then He appeared to James.'* You might ask 'Which James?' There are four men named 'James' in the New Testament. Let us see, briefly, who the other three are.

First, there is James the brother of John, who with his brother became apostles and once were nick-named 'Boanerges, which means Sons of Thunder' (Mark 3:17). James was *'put to death with the sword'* by Herod Agrippa I in AD 44 (Acts 12:2). Jesus had said that James and John would suffer after their mother had asked for a high place in God's glory for them (Mark 10:39). James' brother, John, was exiled to the Isle of Patmos, from where he wrote the book of Revelation under the Holy Spirit's inspiration.

Second, there is another Apostle, James the son of Alphaeus (Matthew 10:3; Acts 1:13). He is also known as *'James the younger'* (Mark 15:40)— or *'James the less'* in some translations. His mother is Mary—not Mary the mother of Jesus, nor Mary Magdalene. (There were a number of Marys, too.)

Third, a man called James is the father of the least known Apostle, Judas, who is not Judas Iscariot (Jesus' betrayer who committed suicide in remorse.) We know this Judas is not Judas Iscariot, who is mentioned separately in the list of the apostles (Luke 6:16).

This leaves us with the fourth James. He met the risen Lord individually, after the 500 brothers had met their resurrected Saviour, but before the apostles met Him (1 Corinthians 15:7). We now concentrate on him and see how God's grace works in a remarkable way!

James, Jude and their physical brother—the Lord Jesus Christ

This James is a physical brother of Jesus Christ (Matthew 13:55; Mark 6:3; Galatians 1:9). He is also Jude's brother. (Jude is also called Judas at times.) Jude wrote a book one chapter long, which bears his name and comes just before the book of Revelation. Jude 1:1 identifies Jude as, *'a servant of Jesus Christ and a brother of James.'* So, James has Mary as his mother—exactly like Jesus, except that James has a human father as well as a human mother. Remember that the virgin Mary conceived Jesus as the Holy Spirit came on her. She commenced sexual relations with her husband only after Jesus was born.

Being in Jesus' physical family could not and did not save James

Remarkable as it is, having Jesus as his brother could not save James or Jude. Everyone needs to repent and trust in Jesus personally as their Saviour and Lord, as God the Holy Spirit works in his or her life. In Mark 3:20–21 Jesus is in a crowded house. As so many are there, that Jesus and His disciples are not 'even able to eat.' His family think Jesus is 'out of His mind' and go to 'take charge of Him.' None of Jesus' brothers are then listed as apostles. There is no hint that James or Jude trust in or follow Jesus at this particular time. They are probably there with all the family, trying to control Jesus. What a bizarre thought, that they thought they knew better than Jesus did! This also reminds us that neither can any of us become a Christian just by being a member of a Christian family: it is a personal relationship with Jesus, through repentance and personal belief in Him, that counts.

Where and when were James and Jude converted?

What changes James and, later, Jude? Risen Jesus meets James— separately from the apostles. Each of the two brothers must, at some time, have come to believe the dual truth of Jesus' resurrection and His death on the cross to forgive and change sinners who turn from sin and trust in Him personally. We are not told when or where that happened. It is vital for any saved person to know now that he or she is saved: where and when are secondary. Sometimes those facts are easily recalled, but sometimes not. The main point is that a new spiritual life in Christ always displays saving faith, even if the person concerned finds it hard to say exactly when and where it happened (2 Corinthians 5:17; Galatians 6:15).

But if Christ takes control of your life, He forgives, cleanses and empowers you to live for Him. Things do change radically. Jude 24–25 show what Jude now thinks and passionately believes about his once rejected brother, Jesus, *'To Him who is able to keep you from falling and to present you before His glorious presence without fault, and with great joy— to the only God our Saviour be glory, majesty, power and authority, through Jesus Christ our Lord, before all ages, now and forevermore! Amen.'* Read all Jude's short letter correcting false teachers who teach error about Jesus and who try to make Christians live sinful lives.

James' life changes dramatically. Who would have thought that God would make a sceptical brother into such a loving follower of Jesus and become such an inspiring leader of fellow Christians?

The Holy Spirit inspires all writers of all the Bible's books. This includes the book of James. It teaches some precious truths, including that *'faith by itself, if it is not accompanied by action, is dead'* (James 2:17). It is not really faith unless it produces a changed lifestyle. Faith is more than mere head belief. 'Even the demons believe [that 'there is one God']—and shudder' (James 2:19). No demon can be saved! You are saved only if you turn from sin, and trust in Jesus by asking him into your heart as your Lord and Saviour.

James, now knowing the risen Jesus as his Saviour, becomes the influential leader and overseer of the entire church in Jerusalem. You will see that is so by reading the answers, given below, to some important questions about the early church. See how God changes, enables and uses a man who trusts in Christ. God makes him a blessing to others. That can, and should, include you!

- Who does the recently converted Paul of Tarsus go to see in Jerusalem to be assured by him that he is on the right road? *James*
- Who are the church's three pillars hearing of the work of Paul and Barnabas with the Gentiles? *James*, Peter and John (in that order).
- Who sends the men to discuss a problem with Paul? *James*

- Who does Peter say should be told when he is freed from jail? *James*
- Who leads the meeting of the leaders and the church about considering the place of Gentiles in the early church? *James*
- Who takes the authority to come to a decision after the discussion in that meeting, and who suggests a plan of action to follow? *James*
- Who is asked for advice about how things should be done? *James*
- Who starts with no confidence in Jesus, along with his family? *James*
- Who is changed entirely by meeting the risen Jesus after He died on the cross to bear his sins and their penalty? *James*
- Who is inspired by God's Holy Spirit to write a book which points out that if you are really saved your life will show it? *James*
- What is the name of that challenging book of five chapters? *James*
- Who do you think historians say sealed his testimony of faith in Christ by being stoned as a martyr in AD 61, by order of the then high priest Ananus, after the procurator, Festus, died? *James*

Encouraging and amazing

Only God's grace can produce such a change in a man who, along with his wider family, is sceptical and does not trust Jesus, much less *trust in Him*. A good church or group leader must first be a soundly converted man, then someone who trusts and obeys the Lord Jesus in everyday life and duties. James obviously finds His understanding of God and spiritual issues growing, to the point where he becomes a member of Jesus' three man 'inner cabinet' and ends up as President of the Council of true believers in the Lord Jesus Christ. Maybe God has a very responsible task or position for you in His plans? You will never be able to do it properly unless you love the Lord with all your heart, mind, soul and strength, and are prepared to love your neighbour—meaning a person in need—as yourself (Luke 10:27). God's grace, that changed an unbelieving physical brother into a truly effective and devoted spiritual brother and child of God, is sufficient for you too. If you become a Christian leader in the days ahead, humbly remember it all started with repentance and faith, and keep living like that and honouring Jesus.

Some final questions for you!

Do *you* realise that Jesus died so you can be forgiven and changed? Do *you* know Jesus dwelling in your heart as your risen and living Lord and Saviour? If so, though not a historic apostolic leader like James, does *your* life bless others now? Are *you* a good and humble example to others? Are *you* prepared to suffer for Christ, if and when that is required of you? Have *you* read the book of James carefully? Have *you* read the book of Jude equally carefully? Are you spending time each day with God in your quiet time of prayer and Bible reading?

Please check the verses on James at the start of this chapter. They support the answers to the questions posed in the above bullet points.

'More than five hundred brothers'

1 CORINTHIANS 15:1–8

The only account

We now see how Jesus' appearing to *'more than five hundred of the brothers at the same time'* fits in with His meeting other people after He died on the cross and rose again from the tomb. Read Paul's letter directed by God the Holy Spirit, in one of the key Bible resurrection passages at 1 Corinthians 15:1–8. Verse 6 contains the only account of the *'five hundred'* (plus!). To have some idea of what preceded and followed this meeting, we now quote verses 5–8: After He rose again, Jesus *'appeared to Peter, and then to the Twelve. 6 After that, he appeared to more than five hundred of the brothers at the same time, most of whom are still living, though some have fallen asleep. 7 Then he appeared to James, then to all the apostles, 8 and last of all he appeared to me also, as to one abnormally born.'* You now can see it in the overall time frame.

Paul neither lists, nor intends to list, each and every post-resurrection appearance of Jesus. He just puts in time order those he chooses to mention. If we had to rely solely on Paul listing every appearance of Jesus, though God could do that if He chose to, someone would say, 'We cannot believe that, because it is just Paul's idea.' We know that the Holy Spirit infallibly inspired and guided every writer of every Bible book to write God's truth, in both the Old and New Testaments. But this real and varied evidence from different witnesses, recorded by five different Spirit-inspired writers, would be accepted as strong in any properly constituted and properly run court of law. Matthew, Mark, Luke, John and Paul record perfectly Jesus' resurrection appearances which God wants us to know about. No doubt, there were others, too, who met Jesus after He died and rose again.

A different way to meet Jesus today

In a different way, we meet Him today when we are sorry for our sins, turn from them from our hearts, and trust Jesus by asking Him into our hearts to dwell there as our living Saviour, through the Holy Spirit. We look back to His death on the cross, where He bore our sins and took the punishment for them in our place. We look forward to experiencing the truth of God's promises that, if we make Jesus at home in our hearts now, He will gladly make us at home forever with Him in Heaven after we die. Until then, He puts within us His free but costly gift of eternal life as we receive Him. (See, John 14:1–6; 3:16; 1 John 5:11–13 and Romans 6:23.) He also indwells every believer in Jesus with His Holy Spirit. Romans 8:5 confirms that, 'if anyone does not have the Spirit of Christ, he does not belong to Christ.'

Limited and chosen witnesses—but good and plenty of them!

Is there a reason why Paul limits his reporting of the Lord Jesus' post-resurrection appearances to Peter (also called 'Cephas'), 'the Twelve' disciples, 'more than five hundred brothers together,' James the brother of Jesus, 'all the apostles,' and 'last of all' Saul of Tarsus (who became the Apostle Paul) in his exceptional experience of meeting the risen Saviour on the Damascus Road? (We will look at Paul in Chapter 9.) The Bible does not reveal why Paul selects these witnesses to write about in the Bible. God does not need to explain to us why Paul or He chose these witnesses. But we know that they are good quality, they are 'first-hand' witnesses all having met the risen Lord Jesus, they corroborate one another, and there are far more of them than would actually be needed in court to establish evidence for the resurrection of Jesus Christ that would convince the court.

Consider the apostles involved

But—apart from *'the five hundred'*—each of Paul's post-risen record in 1 Corinthians 15 clearly involves *apostles*. Each named individual who meets the risen Lord in this passage is, or will become, an apostle. Some apostles are also included in *'the Twelve'* as well as being included in the group together as *'all the apostles,'* It is also likely that more than one apostle is in the crowd of *'more than five hundred brothers.'* Maybe even *all* the apostles are there, except Paul himself who is not converted until after the time he writes about when dealing with the others who saw the risen Lord? In 1 Corinthians 15, Paul may be trying to show that he, along with other true apostles, does meet one of the key requirements for those

God chooses as apostles—namely that an apostle must have met the risen Lord Jesus Christ. In his case, his later meeting the risen Christ on the Damascus Road is unique in how it happened, as we will see in Chapter 9.

Important to understand what an apostle was and did

Why is the question of historic apostleship so important? Because God entrusts to His twelve chosen apostles the leading of the early Church and He gives them His authority to lead. Also, through His apostles, God produces the New Testament Scripture. The Holy Spirit leads the apostles to write the Scriptures, or to supervise closely others who write the Scriptures. It is vital to recognise God's original early church apostles clearly to enable the running of the early Church, and more vital still for the compiling and completion of God's written word, the Bible. God gives them His authority. Paul, when justifying his position and authority as an apostle makes a clear distinction between a Biblical apostle and any other keen disciple of the Lord Jesus Christ.

'The things that mark an apostle'

The apostles are clearly distinguished from other Christians in the book of Acts, which is the most reliable early church history book. The Acts of the Apostles show that authoritative New Testament teaching, always Holy Spirit led and enabled, comes only through the apostles or those under their authority who are in close contact with them and are influenced by them (Acts 2:42). Acts also makes a point of saying that 'many wonders and miraculous signs'—given by God to underline their God-given task and authority—come through the apostles (Acts 2:43). The apostles' preaching and their testimony to the resurrection of Jesus are also marked by 'great power' (Acts 4:33). These are things that distinguish and mark out the unique, one-off, historically God-chosen apostles from all others. So when Paul makes the case to the rebellious Corinthian church that he is a genuine apostle, and therefore has both the authority and duty to instruct them as an apostle, he says, 'The things that mark an apostle—signs, wonders and miracles—were done among you with great perseverance' (2 Corinthians 12:12). He reminds them of the exceptional way that God has used him, always entirely by God's grace alone.

Brothers

We are not told which men are included in the 500 or so 'brothers.' We know it does not mean physical, but spiritual, 'brothers.' John 1:12 tells us that when we really believe in Jesus, and so receive Him into our hearts, we 'become children of God,' and so we are automatically brothers and/or sisters of all others who personally trust in Christ. There are some important reasons why this gathering of 'five hundred brothers or more' is important.

- Verse 6 says that the crucified, but risen, Jesus appeared 'to more than five hundred of the brothers at the same time, most of whom are still living, though some have fallen asleep.' Some have slept the sleep of death on earth and have woken up 'away from the body and at home with the Lord' (2 Corinthians 5:8). This reminds us that our lives are short and uncertain. However, if we know Jesus our future is certain and eternally wonderful with Jesus. Those who have died in Christ have only died a physical death but now they enjoy eternal spiritual life in Heaven 'with the Lord' and will later receive a resurrection body to go with their saved soul! (1 Thessalonians 4:13–18; 2 Thessalonians 1:5–10; 1 Corinthians 15:35–58). If you die today, will you be with Christ forever? Are you sure? You can be. (Please read Romans 10:9–10 and then pray.)
- But most of the 500 are still alive even as 1 Corinthians 15 is being written. To have live witnesses present when the evidence is being presented is particularly persuasive. This principle applies very much to the resurrection of Jesus. It is while the witnesses are alive and present that the early Christians proclaim the risen Christ. They are there to be grilled about it—everyone there knows it occurred.
- As most of Christ's risen appearances are not to large crowds, it greatly underlines the huge weight of evidence that 'more than five hundred' saw Him on this occasion. There is no-one objecting because it is wrong, or fictional. Those who say that people were hallucinating or being manipulated, are already flying in the face of fact. But they cannot explain how 500 people should all get this wrong in the same way and be disillusioned or hallucinate

together, just like varied individuals do in different conditions and numbers, and at different times of day and night! And note the lack of exaggeration—just 'more than' 500 are involved. There is no exaggeration here. And again, most of them are there to be questioned about whether what is written is true!

- This is the biggest early meeting with the risen Christ. But 500 people will make an amazing impact as surely most of them must tell their many friends and family and others what they know that they have all seen. It sets the scene for the 3,000 converts to be baptised on the Day of Pentecost after Peter preaches the gospel of the cross, resurrection, repentance and faith to many people in crowded Jerusalem (Acts 2:14–40, especially verse 40). These people, especially the 500-plus brothers, are prepared by God to hear the gospel, which some of them surely would have done on the Day of Pentecost when Peter preached to them. He then tells them that 'everyone who calls on the name of the Lord will be saved' (Acts 2:21). In that message he stresses what happened at and around the cross, and that Jesus rose from the grave. The ground is truly prepared for faithful sowing and fruitful reaping as Peter sows the word of God. With so many at one time who saw the risen Lord, as well as all the individuals who testify to meeting Jesus, those listening knew that they were being faced with solid facts as well as scriptural truth.

- This reminds those of us who have become 'born again'—always by faith alone in Christ alone—of the need and privilege to share with individuals how we came to know Jesus as our Lord and Saviour, and how He works in the life of every individual who turns from sin to Jesus. We can also see the immense privilege of taking opportunities to speak to larger gatherings and crowds of people as we mature and some of us are given that opportunity. Never be ashamed of Jesus, whether you talk to many or to few! If you are 'born again' and faithful in witnessing to individuals, maybe God has bigger plans for you in the gospel in the days ahead?

'Doubting' Thomas

JOHN 20:19–31

A doubting disposition

We now focus on the Bible's most famous doubter, who sees and meets the risen Lord Jesus Christ and gets converted. Who is that? Thomas! It seems that Thomas always had a doubting disposition. In John 11:7–16, after Jesus tells His disciples, *'Let us go back to Judea,'* they respond with, *'a short while ago the Jews tried to stone You, and yet you are going back there?'* Jesus replies by pointing out that time is short and there He will raise dead Lazarus from the 'sleep' of his physical death. Thomas (whose name 'Didymus' means 'Twin') says, *'Let us also go, that we may die with Him [Jesus].'* Those words demonstrate commendable loyalty to Jesus but show no faith in Christ's ability to keep them all alive or to raise Lazarus! Doubts already play a big part in his thinking.

Previous doubt—and spreading doubt

Do you recall the famous passage in John 14:1–14? Jesus talks about preparing us a home in Heaven and His coming again, and promises, *'I will come back and take you to be with Me that you may also be where I am. You know the way to the place where I am going,'* by which He means that the way to Heaven is by trusting His promise and putting their personal faith in Him. (Just the same for us today!) Thomas replies that they do not know where Jesus is going, *'so how can we know the way?'* Jesus' classic reply shows that the only way to have your sins forgiven, eternal life now, and a Heavenly home forever is by faith alone in Christ alone. He says, *'I am the way and the truth and the life. No one comes to the Father except through Me.'* He then said that to know God the Son, Jesus Himself, means you also get to know God, the Father—showing His unity and equality with the Father in the oneness of the Trinity. (God the Holy Spirit is the third Person in our triune God.)

Thomas' disposition to doubt then spreads to Philip. (It is amazing how someone, even faithful Philip, can take up the doubts of another.) Philip expresses his doubts by saying, *'Lord, show us the Father and that will be enough for us.'* Jesus tells him also to believe both His words and His miracles as evidence of His unity with the Father. But the question here is, 'Who started the doubting?' The answer is, of course, 'Doubting Thomas.' Later He will come to know and experience faith in the Lord Jesus as the only way to God. I found it was only when I actually received the living Lord Jesus Christ as my Saviour, who paid the penalty for my sins, that my experience of Him seemed to illuminate the Bible truth that He alone is the 'Way the truth and the life'.

Disciple and apostle

Thomas is named as a disciple and as an apostle in the three other Gospels and in Acts. But we only hear of him individually in John. The only other references to him are in John 20:19–31, about post-resurrection Jesus appearing twice to the disciples, first without Thomas and then with Thomas. John 20:19–31 is a real and blessed 'must' to read. Please do read it before you carry on reading this chapter.

There are six separate episodes covered in these two appearances of risen Jesus:

1. The disciples blessed: John 20:19–23
2. Thomas missing: John 20:24
3. The disciples share: John 20:25
4. Thomas doubting: John 20:25
5. The disciples have fellowship: John 20:26
6. Thomas believing: John 20:27–29

The disciples blessed: John 20:19–23

It is the first day of the week. In time this day of the week will become the Christian weekly Sabbath rest of one day in seven, but it will celebrate not only God's rest from His six-day creation, but also the day of the Lord Jesus' resurrection from the tomb.

It is evening. The disciples feel very low and meet behind closed doors: they are cowering away because they fear Jewish opposition, probably stirred up by the same religious leaders—the Scribes, Pharisees and High Priests—as those who engineered the crucifixion of their Lord Jesus Christ. The Jews have weaved this web of terror into the hearts of these followers on Christ, who all once claimed they would follow Jesus through thick and thin.

Peter had said to Jesus in front of the disciples, 'Even if all fall away, I will not.' Jesus had replied, 'I tell you the truth, today—yes, tonight—before the cock crows twice you yourself will disown me three times.' We read that then 'Peter insisted emphatically, "Even if I have to die with you, I will never disown you."' But 'all the others said the same.' Peter did deny three times that he even knew Jesus. The cock did crow three times. They all fled.

Into this background of guilt and fear, and through locked doors, 'Jesus came and stood in the midst.' There is no explanation of how the risen Christ does this—just the fact that He comes. Today, He comes into the hearts of those who turn from sin and guilt and trust Him, even where fear, and especially where guilt, exist. Jesus gives no explanation: just turn from sin to Him, and He comes to you, through the Holy Spirit.

Twice Jesus brings His blessed greeting of 'Peace' to them. Jesus brings us peace with our offended God because He suffered God's wrath in His body for us when He was punished in our place on the cross. He gives us the peace of God in our hearts when we receive Him, as the Holy Spirit comes to live within the true believer. And He gives us the message of peace from God to share with all sinners who will repent and trust in Him. (That too is still true today.)

Jesus now shows them His nail-pierced hands and His gashed side: in other words, He reminds them that He has died on the cross for each one of them and that He now lives again! To say they are *'glad when they [see] the Lord'* must be one of the Bible's greatest under-statements! After His second 'Peace' greeting, He recommissions them to go to others with the gospel of forgiveness of sins through faith in Christ, and He promises them His Holy Spirit to do that.

Thomas missing: John 20:24

We simply read, that Thomas 'was not with them when Jesus came.' When Jesus Christ came to save some people you know, did you feel as if you were 'out?' Did you miss out when Christ came to others, bringing His forgiveness for them and a new life of peace, God-enabled living, and purpose to live for Him? Thomas probably feels like that now: he is a stranger and an outsider to being saved from sin or being 'born again.' He is looking in, lost and sceptical, from the outside. He is an outsider at the moment from God's forgiveness, new life, and guaranteed home in Heaven after death (Mark 14:29–31).

The disciples share: John 20:25

The disciples do not use complicated arguments or deep theology at this point. They simply share with Thomas, 'We have seen the Lord.' Sometimes we need to go into detail to others about why we trust the Bible and receive Christ. Christians should be aiming increasingly at *'Always be prepared to give an answer to everyone who asks you to give the* reason for the hope *that you have'* (1 Peter 3:15). At other times sharing a simple statement of Bible truth, or a word of testimony, is all that is then needed. God used a lad with five loaves and two fishes to feed over 5,000 people! (Read Matthew 14:21 and Mark 16:9.) He can use the little that you know about the gospel to feed many sinners with the 'Bread of life' (John 6:35). Just keep trusting Him and sharing His message.

Thomas doubting: John 20:25

Thomas states clearly and stubbornly that, unless he sees and fingers the nail-prints in Jesus' hands and puts his hand into Jesus' speared side, he will not believe. God does nothing immediately. He leaves Thomas to 'stew' for eight days. Often when someone hears the gospel and reacts  against it, God will work on his conscience and heart by His Holy Spirit, even in his quieter moments, until he is ready to respond positively. Before I trusted in Christ, my sister gave me a book titled *Believing Is Seeing*. I never read the book, but I spent hours wondering about the title. When I came to believe in Christ, a little later, I suddenly began to 'see' it all! Those 'dead' moments were used by God to prepare me to respond to the gospel one Saturday night in Leeds. He made me ready to trust in Jesus personally. If you are a Christian, keep praying for your family members, friends and contacts. God may well be at work in their hearts, though you may not know it.

The disciples have fellowship: John 20:26

After eight days, the disciples are in fellowship again, gathered behind closed doors. Jesus comes 'and stood in their midst' again. Unless we harden our hearts too often, Jesus keeps knocking at our hearts' door lovingly. Jesus says in Revelation 3:20, 'Here I am! I stand at the door and knock. If anyone hears my voice and opens the door, I will come in.' But the time may come when we have resisted His voice and offer of grace so much that our hearts become too hardened to even sense that He is there or 'hear' His knocking. Our hearts can become spiritually calloused. Beware! When God speaks to your heart, respond immediately and positively. Again, Jesus says, *'Peace to you.'* But there is a big difference this time: Thomas is now there with the disciples!

Thomas believing: John 20:27–28

Jesus talks personally to Thomas. He also talks to us personally today in our hearts by His word, by His Spirit, by reading the Bible, by hearing the Bible explained in services and Bible studies, and by Christians sharing with us how they came to trust Jesus and what God has done for them since. When Jesus invites Thomas to look at, touch and handle the wounds in His hands and side, there is no record that Thomas does that. He simply replies, *'My Lord and my God!'* Although Thomas is convinced because He sees the evidence that the risen Lord Jesus Christ died on the cross for his sins, Jesus says, *'Blessed are those who have not seen and yet have believed.'* I am one of those many 'blessed' people who have never seen Jesus physically, but believe in Christ, by God's grace. The same is true of all real Christian people living since Jesus ascended to Heaven.

Are you blessed by personal saving faith in Jesus? If not, why not repent of your sins and trust in the risen Jesus, right now? Do what Thomas did: first, realise Jesus really did die in your place and took the judgment for your sins on the cross; then rejoice that He did rise again and lives today; then be prepared to repent of your sins and put the Lord Jesus on the throne of your heart; and then declare Jesus to others as your Lord and your God. If you have not yet done so, do it now! By faith and telling others you have received Christ, you will receive the assurance that God has heard your prayer and saved you (Romans 10:9–10). If you have trusted Christ, thank God, and share this great message of good news with others.

Saul who becomes Paul[1]

ACTS 26:1–19
ALSO REFER TO: ACTS 9:1–19; 22:1–21

New name and new nature

Saul of Tarsus' name and nature change after meeting the risen Lord Jesus Christ. Saul, who becomes Paul, is the last person in our focus on those who meet Jesus after He died and rose again. (In the next and final chapter of this book we will look at the risen Redeemer Himself.) Acts 9:1–19 and 22:1–21 tell what happened, confirmed in Acts 26:8–20. Paul says, 'last of all [Jesus] appeared to me also, as to one abnormally born' (1 Corinthians 15:8). Christ's appearance to Saul differs from all the others: it happens not only after Jesus has died and risen again: it is also after He ascended to Heaven. Before He appears to Saul, Peter's sermon has, by the Holy Spirit, produced 3,000 converts from many nations in packed-out Jerusalem at Pentecost (Acts 2:14–41). God also has transformed many weak and new Christians. (He still does when sinners turn from sins and yield to Jesus Christ as Lord and Saviour.) It was after all this that the glory of the resurrected Jesus outshines the mid-day sun, as He appears to Saul. Paul is both the first and the last of all God's chosen apostles to meet the risen Lord Jesus Christ after His ascension. In fact, he is the only apostle to meet the Lord Jesus Christ after His ascension. It is interesting to note that, as we have seen, when God the Father's hand of punishment fell on His Son in our place on the cross, darkness blotted out the mid-day sun. When God's grace stops Saul, in his persecutions, to become Paul, the brightness and glory of Jesus outshine the mid-day sun as a witness to the conversion of a proud persecutor of the church, who will become an apostle, evangelist, pastor, Bible teacher, and even—by God the Holy Spirit's influence and inspiration—the most prolific writer of New Testament Scripture. He will not only have a huge effect upon Jewish people everywhere—from some of whom he will receive cruel opposition himself—but he will also be the pioneer apostle to the Gentiles. This truly is a most significant time when the risen and ascended Jesus uniquely appears to Saul.

How is Saul changed after meeting the risen Lord Jesus?

After answering this question, we will see what happened to Saul on the road to Damascus. Saul, who will become Paul, is persecuted, and often beaten, thrown into prison, and even stoned by the Jews. Read about the amount and types of Paul's staggering sufferings in 2 Corinthians 11:22–29. The Jews are furious that their anti-Christian persecutor and 'hard man' suddenly becomes a faithful follower of Jesus. Saul was sent by the chief priests to pursue and imprison new Christians, make them 'blaspheme' (by confessing that Jesus is Lord, as well as God the Son, the Son of God, and the Messiah), and even to have them killed. The Jews had caused Jesus to be crucified.

But Saul not only becomes converted: he becomes Paul, a leading Christian apostle! Yet he never becomes anti-Jewish. After he trusts in Christ, God leads him to concentrate on taking the gospel of forgiveness, through faith alone in Jesus Christ alone, to the Gentiles. Still, he keeps his normal practice, immediately on arrival anywhere, to visit the nearest synagogue to meet fellow Jews. He still longs to see his own people come to Jesus for forgiveness. When Jesus bore sinners' sins and took God's punishment for them in His body on the cross, it was for Jews and for Gentiles. (It was also for you and me.) The Christian message is that 'all *have sinned and fall short of the glory of God*' and that God '*commands all people everywhere to repent*' (Romans 6:23; Acts 17:30). That excludes *no one* who will repent and trust Jesus.

He could not have been more Jewish

Philippians 3:4–6 shows just how Jewish Saul was: circumcised according to the Old Testament law; a naturally born Israelite; of the same tribe as Israel's first king, his name-sake, Saul; a fully Hebrew son of Hebrew parents maintaining his Hebrew language in a pagan city; a Pharisee trained by Gamaliel, the leading Pharisee; and meticulously legalistic in keeping the small print of Jewish law and teaching it to others. Saul's zeal made him obsessed to weed out Jews converted to Jesus Christ. No one expected Jesus to stop him in his tracks as he journeyed to Damascus to terrorise Christians! Sometimes Christians ask themselves if it is even possible that one person or another can ever be converted to Christ. It seems so unlikely because some are seemingly so very far away from the remotest chance that they will ever consider the gospel openly, repent of their sins, and turn to Jesus Christ. Will they be honest enough about their sins to know they need God's forgiveness and His power to change them? Will they actually turn from those sins and recognise that the Lord Jesus Christ, God the Son, has been judged on the cross for their sins and will come into their lives to save them, if only they turn to Him by faith alone? My *guess* is that although Saul was on the prayer lists of many keen and devoted Christians, not many of them *really* expected him to become converted. Now there is a lesson for those of us who know the Lord, today, in our increasingly anti-Christian world.

A complete change of life and mind-set

Yet he was and is converted to the Lord Jesus Christ! His whole life and mind-set are changed as Philippians 3:7–11 shows. Now all else seems relatively minor to him compared with *'the surpassing greatness of knowing Jesus Christ.'* He now sees that his boasted 'righteousness,' piled up by self-effort and keeping legalistic rules, is worse than *nothing*. It is *'rubbish'*—in fact that is polite translation of a word that means 'dung.' But that is how Paul now sees self-effort and self-righteousness as a means of saving him! Yet since he turned from sin to trust Jesus, God's perfect righteousness is counted as *his*! He has exchanged his sins for God's gracious forgiveness and His free gift of Christ's righteousness. This is so real to him that he wants to go on knowing Christ better and experiencing His resurrection power through the living Christ dwelling in his heart by the Holy Spirit. He is also willing to suffer for his Saviour. He now wants to live a different 'resurrection life' on earth: that can only be attained daily as he dies to self and sin and is constantly filled by the Holy Spirit each day. For that he must keep looking to Jesus. What an amazing change! The open secret is that, in principle, we can experience the same change as Saul though his details and ours are probably very different. But by God's grace we follow in Saul's footsteps  because we 'fix our eyes on Jesus, the author and perfecter of our faith' (Hebrews 12:2), in constantly turning from our temptations and our sin in order to make Jesus Christ our Lord.

What happens to Saul on the Damascus Road?

The Lord meets Saul just as he is fully occupied with persecuting Christianity and Christians. Here is a summary of his experience taken from the larger record in Acts 26:1–19:

13 About noon, O King, as I was on the road, I saw a light from heaven, brighter than the sun, blazing around me and my companions. 14 We all fell to the ground, and I heard a voice saying to me in Aramaic, 'Saul, Saul, why do you persecute me? It is hard for you to kick against the goads.' 15 Then I asked, 'Who are you, Lord?' 'I am Jesus,

whom you are persecuting,' the Lord replied. 16 'Now get up and stand on your feet. I have appeared to you to appoint you as a servant and as a witness of what you have seen of me and what I will show you. 17 I will rescue you from your own people and from the Gentiles. I am sending you to them 18 to open their eyes and turn them from darkness to light, and from the power of Satan to God, so that they may receive forgiveness of sins and a place among those who are sanctified by faith in me.'

Paul answers a Roman Governor and a King who is a Jewish expert

Paul is now present in an unofficial hearing in Caesarea, which is under Rome's jurisdiction. Festus is the region's Roman Governor. The visiting king, Agrippa, expert on Jewish laws and customs, comes to advise Festus about Paul's case, which the Jews strongly oppose. Paul, though Jewish, is a Roman citizen and has appealed to Caesar in Rome, as is his right under Roman law. Festus must report to Caesar, so the Emperor knows the position fully. Caesar is the most powerful world ruler, who does not 'suffer fools gladly.' Paul *of Tarsus* is unusual being *both* Jewish *and* Roman. He rightly claims he is being judged wrongly for believing in the resurrection from the dead, including Jesus' resurrection. That is not a crime under Roman law. He is asked to speak. He will testify to Agrippa, Festus and a courtroom full of influential people, probably most neutral but some bitterly opposed to Paul. He is going to say how he met the risen Jesus. Paul always seeks to present the gospel wherever he is and whoever he is with—a real challenge to Christians today. He must also justify legally his appeal to Caesar. Resurrection has long been believed in by orthodox Jews, but of course they have already rejected Jesus. Paul also claims the Jews' have *no* evidence to support their false allegations about him. Now we join Saul as he describes to his high-powered audience what happens to him on the Damascus Road.

Saul's bad conscience pricked by God?

Saul has obeyed orders from the chief priests to arrest Jewish Christians fleeing from Israel. He violently opposes anything about *'the name of Jesus of Nazareth'*, as he showed in Jerusalem. Suddenly *'about noon'* he sees *'a light from heaven, brighter than the sun, blazing around'* him and his fellow travellers. They all fall to the ground. A voice in Aramaic (a local language like Hebrew) says, *'Saul, Saul, why do you persecute Me?'* and likens him to an ox kicking against the goad (a pointed stick which is jabbed into an ox to make it keep on pulling the plough behind it). Does Jesus refer to a goad to remind Saul of his bad conscience pricking him because of his ungodly cruelty to Christians? Instantly, Saul knows this voice is from the Lord from Heaven, and replies, *'Who are you, Lord?'* The Lord replies, *'I am Jesus, whom you are persecuting.'* The crucified, risen and ascended King of kings and Lord of lords now seeks Saul! Jesus tells Saul to rise and stand up. (How often does God humble us in conviction of sin so He can lift us up by blessing us?) The Lord Jesus then tells Saul how He wants him to live and the role He has for him. He is to become Christ's *servant* and *witness*. He will witness of what he has *'seen'* (which means 'experienced') of Jesus already. (He is doing that now before Agrippa and Festus.) In future, he must also keep sharing what God shows him.

For today's Christians, that means testifying how we came to trust Jesus as Saviour, showing we know Jesus by how we now live and then sharing with others what we learn each day about God from the Bible. Every *born-again* person should be doing that constantly and be seeking to share the gospel with others.

Special promise from God to Paul

The Lord promises to rescue Saul from constant danger from some Jews (already seeking his life) and Gentiles (who will become Paul's God-given 'target' for sharing the good news about Jesus.) Today, Christians in many countries face danger and death where violent extremism exists, or if the accepted religion cruelly opposes their knowing and following Jesus, and especially so if they share the good news of the cross and resurrection with non-Christians. The presence of danger never means we cannot witness there. Saul knows he will be sent to places where he urgently and often will need the Lord's protection.

But why witness to others worldwide

Why is Saul sent to these people? Why are Christians commanded by Jesus to still go into the whole world to serve Him? The answer is, *'To open their eyes and turn them from darkness to light and from the power of Satan to God.'* If Paul then, or Christians today, will go and make clear the saving message of the cross and the resurrection, and of repentance and faith, the Holy Spirit will do His work in their hearts, through His servants, to open their spiritual eyes, to turn them from darkness to light, and to deliver them from Satan to God. Jesus says His whole purpose is, *'So they may receive forgiveness of sins and a place among those who are sanctified by faith in Me'.* When sinners have their eyes of understanding opened, turn from sin to receive Jesus, and so also receive God's delivering power, they become God's special children (John 1:12). They become part of His earthly church at once. After death they will be forever in Heaven with Christ and with each person who has ever been saved by faith in Lord Jesus. He gives them *'a place among those who are sanctified [set apart] by faith in Me'.*

Are *you* among them? I do hope so. It is urgent and vital. There is nothing more important than to know sins forgiven, peace with God, and a home in Heaven with the Lord Jesus Christ.

NOTES

1 There is no specific statement in the Bible that Saul's name was changed to Paul as a result of his Damascus Road experience of meeting the Lord Jesus Christ. In this he is unlike, for

example, Abram becoming Abraham, or Jacob becoming Israel. But like Jacob he continued from time to time to be called by his 'first' name. The fact remains that after the Spirit-filled apostle had dealt with Elymas, the sorcerer, and then went with his missionary team to Perga and then Antioch in Syria, he was only called 'Paul', except when recounting his experience on the Damascus Road. The change was not immediate, but it certainly caught on!

The resurrected Redeemer

2 CORINTHIANS 5:14–21; ROMANS 14:7–9; 1 CORINTHIANS 6:19–20 (NIV)

The focus of our attention

I magine a guest of honour being ignored at a dinner specially given for him.

So often we ignore Jesus on His 'special' occasions and instead focus and talk about so many other things, except Him. We talk about ourselves, our jobs, our finances, our sports teams, our entertainments and pleasures, and many other things—some of which are not wrong in themselves. But, even on what we regard as His 'special, days', many people rarely concentrate on Jesus. So, the good news of Christ's death and resurrection is not shared as it should be with non-Christians, who desperately need Jesus. And Christians are not as helped and encouraged as they should be by fellowship, and discussion about the Bible and about God.

This book has focused on people at the cross who saw Jesus die, and on those who met Jesus after the resurrection. Obviously, Jesus is the one who is always involved, but now we will focus our attention on our 'resurrected Redeemer' Himself. He always must be the number one in our lives even though we obviously have to deal with many other necessary matters in life too.

If you know Jesus as your Saviour, you know we will be in Heaven with Him. When you get there, you will discover that Jesus is Heaven's focal point as *'Worthy is the Lamb'* rings out in joy and triumph. But let us centre our thoughts and worship on Him here on earth too, whenever we can.

Our approach in this final chapter is very simple and, I hope, will prove helpful. We are going to consider something about Jesus Himself contained in the other nine chapters of Part 2 where we explored the resurrection.

We started in Chapter 1 to establish some biblical principles about the cross and resurrection, and then glean from each chapter something about who Jesus is, and what He does and has done. Our main focus is not now on the *people* who saw Jesus die on the cross or met Him after He rose from the grave. It is mainly on our cruelly crucified Saviour who did rise again in great triumph from the grave. We will have a 'Focus' on *Him* from each chapter in Part 2.

Focus 1. Setting the Scene to focus on our 'resurrected Redeemer'

Please read Romans 14:7–9 and 2 Corinthians 5:14–21 before you read on in this book. Both passages move from the death and resurrection of the Lord Jesus Christ, to what that means to us and what we should do about it. We do not look at Christ's death and rising again as an antique collector looks at an antique mirror in a shop. We look *into* the mirror of God's word, see Him there, and see ourselves and how we should respond to '*the Son of God, who* loved me and gave himself for me' (Galatians 2:20; see also Galatians 1:4 and Titus 2:4). You may still need to come to know the Lord Jesus as your personal Lord and Saviour. If you have already trusted Christ, your response may well be to worship Him, thank Him, say and mean 'Sorry' to Him and repent. We all need to ask Him to be Lord of our lives day by day, hour by hour, minute by minute, and moment by moment.

From Romans 14:7–9, when we see that Jesus has bought us for Himself and for our salvation, we follow by grace in His loving footsteps. Just as He did not please Himself, so we are to '*live to the Lord*' and one day '*die to the Lord.*' He deserves to be our Lord: we do not deserve to be His servants, but by grace we are. '*We belong to the Lord.*' Part of 1 Corinthians 5:19–20 reiterates this theme: '*You are not your own; you were bought at a price.*' And what a price Jesus paid! He paid that price to own, use, and bless us now and throughout eternity. That is why Romans 14:9 (for me, the key verse in the Bible) says, *'For this very reason, Christ died and returned to life so that He might be Lord of both the dead and the living.'*

2 Corinthians 5:14–21 tells us how our understanding of that works out. Verses 14–15 provides its own commentary and reminds us, 'For Christ's love compels us, because we are convinced that one died for all, and therefore all died. And he died for all, that those who live should no longer live for themselves but for him who died for them and was raised again.'

One hymn challenges us with the words:

All for Jesus. All for Jesus.
All my being's ransomed powers.

Remember 1 Corinthians 6:19–20, 'You *are not your own ... you were bought at a price; therefore glorify God in your body and in your spirit, which are God's.'*

2 Corinthians 5:16 reminds us that we do not now regard Jesus in the same way that the world regards its heroes such as Julius Caesar, Napoleon, Churchill, Roosevelt, Einstein or Kennedy. Jesus, of course, outperforms all of them—He is sinless, perfect and also the incarnate God, so it really is no contest! But we do not see Him now just as a man doing amazing miracles and giving unbeatable teaching. We now see our 'resurrected Redeemer' from the point of view of the *spiritual* blessing of salvation. He gives that to all who turn from sin and trust in Him. The gospel changes each of us who put our trust in His shed blood. He was judged for our sins, rose and lives forever. *'Therefore, if anyone is in Christ, he is a new creation; the old has gone, the new has come.'* Through His death and resurrection, He begins to change us entirely from the inside out when we receive Him!

But our 'resurrected Redeemer' is the Reconciler! He took humanity's hand with one nail-pierced hand, and God's Divine hand with His other.

He has brought together the omnipotent, holy God with unworthy sinners who repent and believe in Him. Jesus wants others to be reconciled to God too, in order to save them from Hell and spend Heaven with them. He also wants reconciled sinners to be reconcilers. With His gift of eternal life, He has given us *the ministry of reconciliation* and told us how to do it! Verses 20–21, *'We implore you on Christ's behalf: Be reconciled to God. God made Him, who had no sin to be sin for us, so that in Him we might become the righteousness of God.'* We should keep that aim constantly in mind and *'Just do it.'* Others need to hear the gospel from your lips, in exactly the same way that you needed to hear it from those who told you to turn from the wrong in your life and ask God for forgiveness and Christ to enter your life.

Focus 2. Learn about our 'resurrected Redeemer' from the women

We might think that these brave, faithful, kind, generous and loving women, whom we met in Chapter 2 of Part 2 of this book, would not only be at the cross when Jesus died, but later would also meet the 'resurrected Redeemer.' I think we would all say that they deserved that. More surprisingly, their kind actions and careful planning become a strong strand of evidence to show that Jesus really died and then rose bodily again from the borrowed tomb of Joseph of Arimathea. So never underestimate the 'co-lateral' value of loving and kind attention and service to and for Jesus, such as these women showed both at the cross and at the empty tomb, and through encouraging other Christians who were struggling.

One thing about our 'resurrected Redeemer' really strikes me here. It shows that Jesus cares for each individual. *He knows our names.* If you trust in Him as your Saviour, your name is on His Heavenly register, known as 'the Lamb's book of life' (Revelation 21:27). It is by far the most important register to have your name on.

I am bad at remembering names, but I know how positively some people respond when I do remember their name correctly. (That is especially so in prisons.) Jesus, of course, is good at names and *everything else*! He knows how we all like to be recognised by name, especially by someone we admire greatly. I recall a ministers' conference where, in the dark, a well-known American preacher and teacher, the guest speaker at the conference, walked past a relatively 'unknown' and unseen man who was talking to some friends. This preacher reaches thousands each week, so could easily forget the names of some relatively 'unknown' people. (None of us are unknown to the Lord, of course!) Out of the dark night the friendly American drawl sounded, 'Is that you, Michael?' (Not his real name.) 'Michael' recognised the speaker's voice, as he often listened to him preach on the 'Web' and knew him well. That greeting really perked him up!

That was just another man lovingly greeting a friend however well-known and gifted he was. But picture Mary Magdalene in John 20:16. She went in early morning darkness to the tomb to treat Jesus' body with spices. She earlier saw Joseph of Arimathea and Nicodemus place Jesus' body in that tomb. The tomb is now open and empty, except for the graveclothes, and the guards have left. She goes to tells Simon Peter and John that someone has taken Jesus' corpse. The two men run to the tomb. They inspect it. There is no body in the tomb. Mary weeps outside the empty tomb. Where have they taken her Lord? She sees and talks with the two angels, explaining her confusion and sadness. She turns round and sees someone she thinks is the gardener. He seems to have appeared suddenly from nowhere. She does not recognise him as Jesus. Maybe her tears make it hard for her to see, or perhaps Jesus hides His identity. But it is the risen Jesus! The supposed gardener asks, *'Woman, why are you crying? Who is it you are looking for?'* Mary fails to recognise Jesus, even when He speaks to her. She says *'Sir, if you have carried Him away, tell me where you have put Him, and I will get Him.'*

Then Jesus says to her one word that changes everything—not because of the word itself, but because of who says it. Our 'resurrected Redeemer' says, *'Mary.'* She replies, in Aramaic, *'Rabboni'*—meaning *'Teacher.'* Jesus tells her not to hold Him physically as He has not yet returned to His Father—He wants her relationship with Him from now on to be solely spiritual and based on faith, not on sight or feeling. Jesus says, *'Go instead to my brothers and tell them, "I am returning to my Father and your Father, to my God and your God."'* She goes and tells them, *'I have seen the Lord.'*

That one word, *'Mary,'* makes such a difference to her. Our Redeemer spoke to many thousands in His ministry. The gospel of His saving love will soon save 3,000 in one day at Pentecost. But He cares for one sad and confused lady and calls her by name to bless her, and at once uses her as His messenger.

Our Saviour cares for and loves individual people. That includes you! Make sure you trust and follow Him too. He not only revives you. He also wants to work with you and use you.

Focus 3. What we learn about our 'resurrected Redeemer' from Peter

In Chapter 3 of Part 2 as we considered Peter, we saw how the risen Lord Jesus deals with failures, like Peter. Just as 'the word of the LORD came to Jonah a second time' (Jonah 2:1), after the prophet had disobeyed God and fled from his duty, so Jesus personally restores Peter, recommissions him, empowers him and mightily uses him. Peter did not become perfect overnight—and neither will you until you get to Heaven! But he was blessed. His fellowship with God and with his fellow Christians was restored. His influence on others, through the Holy Spirit of course, was immense.

Have you stumbled or given up? Pray David's Psalm 51 and keep on keeping on. Your 'resurrected Redeemer' has never left you and never will!

Chapter 10

Focus 4. What we can learn from the two travellers about our 'resurrected Redeemer'

The two travellers, going from Jerusalem to Emmaus, feature in Part 2, Chapter 4.

They met the disguised 'resurrected Redeemer' and walk with Him until they stop for a meal. When He breaks bread, they recognise Him and then He vanishes from their sight. But He does something very basic and helpful for them, and still does it today for us. He still blesses us today in the same way.

Although He is resurrected, He does not just use 'resurrection power' to help them. He goes straight to the written word of God and explains to them from the Scriptures all the things in there which are about Him—the prophecies, promises and pictures of Him in other Old Testament events. This is what the 'resurrected Redeemer' does for those who know Him. He does that today, too. God does not use a 'hotline' to speak to us. He continues to speak to us from His written word. But now we have the New Testament as well as the Old Testament, which together form our Bible. Jesus uses the Old Testament to help the travellers. Old and New were both written by men of God but, far more important, were written without fault under the influence and inspiration of God the Holy Spirit. These two men had been miserable, downcast, and had lost hope. That was all because after Jesus died, they forgot His clear promises that He would be raised from the dead. But Jesus has just opened the word of God to them. He has also opened their eyes of understanding and their hearts. They are changed by that. They now want to tell the disciples they have met the risen Jesus. They go and do so. What a difference it makes to meet and trust Jesus, the 'resurrected Redeemer.' That blessing continues for us each day as we pray to God to open the Bible to us, to help us understand it, and to put it into practice.

Focus 5. How the disciples relate to our 'resurrected Redeemer'

There are many disciples who meet the risen Redeemer. Chapter 5 of Part 2 details what those occasions are, and that will not be repeated now. Instead, we will consider one important thing about our relationship with the Lord Jesus Christ today, based on an important principle we see about the disciples. It is simple but particularly important. It covers three situations: first, disciples all in one group; second, disciples in twos and threes and smaller groups; and third, individual disciples on their own.

It is simply this.

You will not be a blessing to other 'disciples' of Jesus—and remember, all committed born-again people are 'disciples'—unless you are personally surrendered to Christ each day. That includes staying close to Him by having your daily quiet time of prayer and reading and meditating on the Bible. Do not miss a day!

If you cultivate fellowship with individual Christians, preferably men with men, and women with women, *such as twos and threes or even bigger*, that will help you immensely and help you to bless others. Our closest friends should be our fellow Christians. So why not agree to meet up and pray with one or two you know belong to the Lord. Where there are only two or three Christians meeting, Jesus is there. He is the living 'resurrected Redeemer' and will never leave us alone or forsake us. He is 'Immanuel'— that means 'God with us.'

But we Christians need *to all meet together* as believers in our churches and fellowships, and not forsake that, as some do (Hebrews 10:26). The illustration often used is that a fire will glow for a long time, but if you take one glowing coal off the fire and put it in the hearth, it will go dim and cold very much sooner. God meant us to worship together and to fellowship together so we can keep our spiritual warmth and glow together. If you are going on with the Lord, you will also meet regularly with your fellow believers. The Lord's Day, Sunday, is a God-given opportunity to concentrate on Jesus, His work on the cross, and His risen life together in worship. On weekdays, get to the Bible studies whenever possible, as you strengthen and help each other. Go to the prayer meetings too. It is said that 'those who pray together, stay together.'

Disciples need all of this concentration on going on with our 'resurrected Redeemer' and winning others for Him.

Focus 6. What James teaches us about our 'resurrected Redeemer'

We learn a lot about the influence of the crucified, but risen, Jesus Christ when we focus on His physical brother, James, who became His spiritual brother too! We looked at the facts in Chapter 6 of Part 2. Now we concentrate on James' brother, the Lord Jesus Christ.

There are two families we can be involved in: our physical family of mother, father, and however many children are involved. That is God's only kind of physical family—one man, one woman, married for life, caring for and training up any children who come along. Do you remember that James and Jude were in that kind of family with Jesus? But they were not then Christians. We can only get to know Jesus spiritually, and be in His family, if we become 'born again.' But Jesus wants us to win our families for Christ. So, live a godly and loving life for God at home.

We need to realise that our *spiritual* family can only be entered because Jesus has 'redeemed' us, that is, He bought us back from our sins by taking our punishment on the cross, and because we have received Him spiritually in our lives by the Holy Spirit. That can only be because He conquered sin in His death on the cross and overcame the grave when He rose from it!

Members of our *physical* family may oppose family members who insist that they also must be 'born again'—but that is what Jesus taught. But when members of the physical family trust in Jesus they become one with everyone else from their family who trust Jesus. Even those who once opposed Jesus, often come to love Him and revere Him as their Saviour and Lord. It is a great testimony to God's grace that James, who like his physical family resisted Jesus, now follows Him closely and treats Him with loving reverence and respect. It is James' servant-heartedness that helps him become a good leader. That is because of his relationship with his 'resurrected Redeemer,'

Focus 7. 'More than five hundred brothers' with one 'resurrected Redeemer'

We now consider a simple reminder here from Part 2, Chapter 7. It is that, while Jesus cares for and saves individual sinners one by one, He also has a heart for the crowds to know Him. Over 500 brothers meet Christ at the same time. Whether or not they were brothers in Christ when the 500-plus men first met together, we do not know. They certainly were 'brothers' in Christ by the time Paul wrote about them to the Corinthian church.

Our 'resurrected Redeemer' had compassion on the crowd. He saw them as a shepherdless flock. Matthew 6:34 tells us that Jesus once 'saw a large crowd, he had compassion on them, because they were like sheep without a shepherd. So, he began teaching them many things' (Matthew 6:34). It is highly significant that Jesus' response to their need was to teach them His truth. We still need to know and use God's word to fight falsehood, as did our 'resurrected Redeemer.' This lost crowd had no direction, no protection and could easily be prey to predators.

Similarly today, crowds of people who are without Jesus as their Shepherd and Saviour lack purpose, are open to life's problems without having Christ to help them through, and can be influenced by false teachers who will lead them not to Heaven but to Hell. Jesus said, in Mark 7:15, that those *'false prophets'* are like *'ferocious'* wolves in sheep's clothing. He said we should *'watch out'* for them. Never underestimate the vicious damage to lives that false teaching can bring. Urge people to know Christ and search the Scriptures humbly and daily, with the prayer that God the Holy Spirit will guide and bless.

May our 'resurrected Redeemer' give us the heart to reach many and the love and ability to lead individuals to faith in Christ, and to go on with Him. May He give us His grace to help us to get to know His word better and to teach it simply and clearly to others.

Focus 8. How 'Doubting' Thomas is blessed by our 'resurrected Redeemer'

We learn something important about the Lord Jesus' gospel priorities through Thomas coming to the point where he can say of Christ crucified and risen from the dead, *'My Lord and my God.'* In 1 Corinthians 15:3–4 Paul insists that *'what I received I passed on to you as of first importance: that Christ died for our sins according to the Scriptures, that he was buried, that he was raised on the third day according to the Scriptures.'* Did you notice that the risen Christ's gospel is built on three main foundations: first that *'Christ died for our sins;'* second that *'He was raised on the third day;'* and third, that both of those are consistent with what the Bible both proclaims and prophesies, in other words the death of Jesus on the cross and His new life after His resurrection are both *'according to the Scriptures.'* In the case of 'doubting' Thomas we see how that works out in practice.

> " I am the resurrection and the life. The one who believes in me will live, even though they die."
>
> John 11:25.

We all know Thomas is a born doubter. He declares His doubts openly to others after they say that Jesus appeared to his fellow disciples when Thomas was not present. Then, eight days later, Thomas joins with the disciples again and Jesus enters through a closed door in full view of all the disciples including Thomas. Thomas sees the nail prints of crucifixion that Jesus suffered, and declares 'My Lord and my God.' So, what has our risen Lord done? By showing His hands, feet and pierced side to them, Jesus effectively proclaims His crucifixion. By being there and entering through the closed door He demonstrates that He is risen. Here is an acted outworking of the two main tenets of the gospel, Christ's substitutionary death and the miraculous resurrection of the Lord Jesus Christ. We know these were predicted in Scripture's prophecies (for example, Isaiah 52:13—54:12) and they were fulfilled exactly as stated. Here is history written in advance.

As we saw with the two travellers, the risen Jesus did not use His exceptional resurrection power to prove His point by 'zapping' them! He went straight back to the Scriptures to back up His death and resurrection. That is a huge lesson to learn from our 'resurrected Redeemer:' 'Preach the Word' (1 Timothy 4:2).

We also see that Jesus' sense of timing is always perfect and dovetails perfectly with God the Father's will. After the first appearance of Jesus to the disciples without Thomas, the Lord gives Thomas eight days to think things through, as God the Holy Spirit works on Him. Then when the resurrected Jesus appears, Thomas is ready to see the evidence for the resurrection and trust in Christ. God controls His own timetable. Psalm 31:15 says, 'My times are in your hands.'

Focus 9. How our 'resurrected Redeemer' causes Saul to become Paul

Many books have been written about how the risen Lord Jesus revealed Himself to others through the conversion, life, preaching, teaching and service of the apostle Paul. But to conclude this last chapter of Part 2 of this book, I am only going to look briefly at a small part of Acts 26:9–18, to see what the risen Jesus does on that Emmaus Road to cause Saul to become Paul. God, who changes Saul's name and nature, can change your name (to 'Christian') and nature (by your being born again and thus becoming a new creation in Christ).

We know it is the *Lord Jesus* who appears to Saul, prostrates him, talks to him, and saves him. How do we know? Verse 15 Jesus says, *'I am Jesus, whom you are persecuting.'* This is in reply to Saul's asking Him, *'Who are you, Lord?'* after he, and his companions were dazzled by a staggeringly bright light, were thrown to the ground, and the voice asked, *'Saul, Saul, why do you persecute me? It is hard for you to kick against the goads.'*

How does our 'resurrected Redeemer' appear to Saul?

In a dazzling bright light from heaven, blazing around his companions and himself. God the Son, the Creator, is brighter and more powerful even than the sun He made. No other religious leader dare say that! The glory of Jesus *is* the glory of God, simply because *He is God*. God is at work when our risen Lord and Saviour is at work:

- By a voice from Heaven reaching down to earth. As the Lord of Heaven and earth, our 'King of kings and Lord of lords' speaks from His heavenly home to the world from which He seeks to save sinners from sin, death and Hell.

- By replying to sincere questions, even from this extreme rebel who has venomously hated Christ and His people. Our risen Lord wants to save His enemies, and He will if they repent from sin and trust in Him.

- By working on sinners' consciences. For Saul, the pricking of his conscience under God's influence will drive him forward to turn from his sins and trust and serve Jesus. Note that Jesus says it is hard for Saul to *'kick against the goads.'* The word is *'goads.'* not just *'goad.'* There were many occasions when God worked on Saul's conscience. Do you have a nagging conscience over sin? If so, confess it, forsake it, and seek Christ's cleansing and restoration. Do it *now*!

- By giving promises of His good and gracious dealings to the man about to become a Christian.
- By giving Him the most important task in the world—to turn sinners from Satan's power, to open their eyes and enlighten them, to rescue them from Satan's power, to know forgiveness, and to enable them to receive an eternal inheritance in Heaven along with all others whose are Christ's by faith.

The most fitting sentence to complete this book is from the timeless hymn, 'Man of Sorrows'. It is:

'Hallelujah! What a Saviour!'

Scripture passages referred to in Parts 1 and 2 (NIV)

Isaiah 52

13 See, my servant will act wisely; he will be raised and lifted up and highly exalted. 14 Just as there were many who were appalled at him—his appearance was so disfigured beyond that of any man and his form marred beyond human likeness—15 so will he sprinkle many nations, and kings will shut their mouths because of him. For what they were not told, they will see, and what they have not heard, they will understand.

Isaiah 53

1 Who has believed our message and to whom has the arm of the LORD been revealed? 2 He grew up before him like a tender shoot, and like a root out of dry ground. He had no beauty or majesty to attract us to him, nothing in his appearance that we should desire him. 3 He was despised and rejected by men, a man of sorrows, and familiar with suffering. Like one from whom men hide their faces he was despised, and we esteemed him not.

4 Surely he took up our infirmities and carried our sorrows, yet we considered him stricken by God, smitten by him, and afflicted. 5 But he was pierced for our transgressions, he was crushed for our iniquities; the punishment that brought us peace was upon him, and by his wounds we are healed. 6 We all, like sheep, have gone astray, each of us has turned to his own way; and the LORD has laid on him the iniquity of us all. 7 He was oppressed and afflicted, yet he did not open his mouth; he was led like a lamb to the slaughter, and as a sheep before her shearers is silent, so he did not open his mouth. 8 By oppression and judgment he was taken away. And who can speak of his descendants? For he was cut

off from the land of the living; for the transgression of my people he was stricken. 9 He was assigned a grave with the wicked, and with the rich in his death, though he had done no violence, nor was any deceit in his mouth.

10 Yet it was the LORD's will to crush him and cause him to suffer, and though the LORD makes his life a guilt offering, he will see his offspring and prolong his days, and the will of the LORD will prosper in his hand. 11 After the suffering of his soul, he will see the light *of life* and be satisfied; by his knowledge my righteous servant will justify many, and he will bear their iniquities. 12 Therefore I will give him a portion among the great, and he will divide the spoils with the strong, because he poured out his life unto death, and was numbered with the transgressors. For he bore the sin of many, and made intercession for the transgressors.

Matthew 26

14 Then one of the twelve, called Judas Iscariot, went to the chief priests 15 and said, "What are you willing to give me if I deliver Him to you?" And they counted out to him thirty pieces of silver. 16 So from that time he sought opportunity to betray Him.

17 Now on the first *day* of the *Feast of* the Unleavened Bread the disciples came to Jesus, saying to Him, "Where do You want us to prepare for You to eat the Passover?" 18 And He said, "Go into the city to a certain man, and say to him, 'The Teacher says, "My time is at hand; I will keep the Passover at your house with My disciples."'" 19 So the disciples did as Jesus had directed them; and they prepared the Passover. 20 When evening had come, He sat down with the twelve. 21 Now as they were eating, He said, "Assuredly, I say to you, one of you will betray Me." 22 And they were exceedingly sorrowful, and each of them began to say to Him, "Lord, is it I?" 23 He answered and said, "He who dipped *his* hand with Me in the dish will betray Me. 24 "The Son of Man indeed goes just as it is written of Him, but woe to that man by whom the Son of Man is betrayed! It would have

been good for that man if he had not been born." 25 Then Judas, who was betraying Him, answered and said, "Rabbi, is it I?" He said to him, "You have said it."

26 And as they were eating, Jesus took bread, blessed and broke *it*, and gave *it* to the disciples and said, "Take, eat; this is My body." 27 Then He took the cup, and gave thanks, and gave *it* to them, saying, "Drink from it, all of you. 28 "For this is My blood of the new covenant, which is shed for many for the remission of sins. 29 "But I say to you, I will not drink of this fruit of the vine from now on until that day when I drink it new with you in My Father's kingdom." 30 And when they had sung a hymn, they went out to the Mount of Olives.

31 Then Jesus said to them, "All of you will be made to stumble because of Me this night, for it is written: 'I will strike the Shepherd, And the sheep of the flock will be scattered.' 32 "But after I have been raised, I will go before you to Galilee." 33 Peter answered and said to Him, "Even if all are made to stumble because of You, I will never be made to stumble." 34 Jesus said to him, "Assuredly, I say to you that this night, before the rooster crows, you will deny Me three times." 35 Peter said to Him, "Even if I have to die with You, I will not deny You!" And so said all the disciples.

36 Then Jesus came with them to a place called Gethsemane, and said to the disciples, "Sit here while I go and pray over there." 37 And He took with Him Peter and the two sons of Zebedee, and He began to be sorrowful and deeply distressed. 38 Then He said to them, "My soul is exceedingly sorrowful, even to death. Stay here and watch with Me." 39 He went a little farther and fell on His face, and prayed, saying, "O My Father, if it is possible, let this cup pass from Me; nevertheless, not as I will, but as You *will*." 40 Then He came to the disciples and found them asleep, and said to Peter, "What? Could you not watch with Me one hour? 41 "Watch and pray, lest you enter into temptation. The spirit indeed *is* willing, but the flesh *is* weak." 42 Again, a second time, He went away and prayed, saying, "O My Father, if this cup cannot pass away from Me unless I drink it, Your

will be done." 43 And He came and found them asleep again, for their eyes were heavy. 44 So He left them, went away again, and prayed the third time, saying the same words. 45 Then He came to His disciples and said to them, "Are *you* still sleeping and resting? Behold, the hour is at hand, and the Son of Man is being betrayed into the hands of sinners. 46 "Rise, let us be going. See, My betrayer is at hand."

47 And while He was still speaking, behold, Judas, one of the twelve, with a great multitude with swords and clubs, came from the chief priests and elders of the people. 48 Now His betrayer had given them a sign, saying, "Whomever I kiss, He is the One; seize Him." 49 Immediately he went up to Jesus and said, "Greetings, Rabbi!" and kissed Him. 50 But Jesus said to him, "Friend, why have you come?" Then they came and laid hands on Jesus and took Him. 51 And suddenly, one of those *who were* with Jesus stretched out *his* hand and drew his sword, struck the servant of the high priest, and cut off his ear. 52 But Jesus said to him, "Put your sword in its place, for all who take the sword will perish by the sword. 53 "Or do you think that I cannot now pray to My Father, and He will provide Me with more than twelve legions of angels? 54 "How then could the Scriptures be fulfilled, that it must happen thus?" 55 In that hour Jesus said to the multitudes, "Have you come out, as against a robber, with swords and clubs to take Me? I sat daily with you, teaching in the temple, and you did not seize Me. 56 "But all this was done that the Scriptures of the prophets might be fulfilled." Then all the disciples forsook Him and fled.

57 And those who had laid hold of Jesus led *Him* away to Caiaphas the high priest, where the scribes and the elders were assembled. 58 But Peter followed Him at a distance to the high priest's courtyard. And he went in and sat with the servants to see the end. 59 Now the chief priests, the elders, and all the council sought false testimony against Jesus to put Him to death, 60 but found none. Even though many false witnesses came forward, they found none. But at last two false witnesses came forward 61 and said, "This

fellow said, 'I am able to destroy the temple of God and to build it in three days.' " 62 And the high priest arose and said to Him, "Do You answer nothing? What *is it* these men testify against You?" 63 But Jesus kept silent. And the high priest answered and said to Him, "I put You under oath by the living God: Tell us if You are the Christ, the Son of God!" 64 Jesus said to him, "*It is as* you said. Nevertheless, I say to you, hereafter you will see the Son of Man sitting at the right hand of the Power, and coming on the clouds of heaven." 65 Then the high priest tore his clothes, saying, "He has spoken blasphemy! What further need do we have of witnesses? Look, now you have heard His blasphemy! 66 "What do you think?" They answered and said, "He is deserving of death." 67 Then they spat in His face and beat Him; and others struck *Him* with the palms of their hands, 68 saying, "Prophesy to us, Christ! Who is the one who struck You?"

69 Now Peter sat outside in the courtyard. And a servant girl came to him, saying, "You also were with Jesus of Galilee." 70 But he denied it before *them* all, saying, "I do not know what you are saying." 71 And when he had gone out to the gateway, another *girl* saw him and said to those *who were* there, "This *fellow* also was with Jesus of Nazareth." 72 But again he denied with an oath, "I do not know the Man!" 73 And a little later those who stood by came up and said to Peter, "Surely you also are *one* of them, for your speech betrays you." 74 Then he began to curse and swear, *saying*, "I do not know the Man!" Immediately a rooster crowed. 75 And Peter remembered the word of Jesus who had said to him, "Before the rooster crows, you will deny Me three times." So he went out and wept bitterly.

Matthew 27

1 Early in the morning, all the chief priests and the elders of the people came to the decision to put Jesus to death. 2 They bound him, led him away and handed him over to Pilate, the governor. 3 When Judas, who had betrayed him, saw that Jesus was condemned, he was seized with remorse and returned the thirty silver coins to the chief priests and the

elders. 4 "I have sinned," he said, "for I have betrayed innocent blood." "What is that to us?" they replied. "That's your responsibility." 5 So Judas threw the money into the temple and left. Then he went away and hanged himself. 6 The chief priests picked up the coins and said, "It is against the law to put this into the treasury, since it is blood money." 7 So they decided to use the money to buy the potter's field as a burial place for foreigners. 8 That is why it has been called the Field of Blood to this day. 9 Then what was spoken by Jeremiah the prophet was fulfilled: "They took the thirty silver coins, the price set on him by the people of Israel, 10 and they used them to buy the potter's field, as the Lord commanded me."

11 Meanwhile Jesus stood before the governor, and the governor asked him, "Are you the king of the Jews?" "Yes, it is as you say," Jesus replied. 12 When he was accused by the chief priests and the elders, he gave no answer. 13 Then Pilate asked him, "Don't you hear the testimony they are bringing against you?" 14 But Jesus made no reply, not even to a single charge—to the great amazement of the governor. 15 Now it was the governor's custom at the Feast to release a prisoner chosen by the crowd. 16 At that time they had a notorious prisoner, called Barabbas. 17 So when the crowd had gathered, Pilate asked them, "Which one do you want me to release to you: Barabbas, or Jesus who is called Christ?" 18 For he knew it was out of envy that they had handed Jesus over to him. 19 While Pilate was sitting on the judge's seat, his wife sent him this message: "Don't have anything to do with that innocent man, for I have suffered a great deal today in a dream because of him." 20 But the chief priests and the elders persuaded the crowd to ask for Barabbas and to have Jesus executed. 21 "Which of the two do you want me to release to you?" asked the governor. "Barabbas," they answered. 22 "What shall I do, then, with Jesus who is called Christ?" Pilate asked. They all answered, "Crucify him!" 23 "Why? What crime has he committed?" asked Pilate. But they shouted all the louder, "Crucify him!" 24 When Pilate saw that he was getting nowhere, but that instead an uproar was starting, he took water and

washed his hands in front of the crowd. "I am innocent of this man's blood," he said. "It is your responsibility!" 25 All the people answered, "Let his blood be on us and on our children!"

26 Then he released Barabbas to them. But he had Jesus flogged, and handed him over to be crucified. 27 Then the governor's soldiers took Jesus into the Praetorium and gathered the whole company of soldiers round him. 28 They stripped him and put a scarlet robe on him, 29 and then twisted together a crown of thorns and set it on his head. They put a staff in his right hand and knelt in front of him and mocked him. "Hail, king of the Jews!" they said. 30 They spat on him, and took the staff and struck him on the head again and again. 31 After they had mocked him, they took off the robe and put his own clothes on him. Then they led him away to crucify him. 32 As they were going out, they met a man from Cyrene, named Simon, and they forced him to carry the cross.

33 They came to a place called Golgotha (which means The Place of the Skull). 34 There they offered Jesus wine to drink, mixed with gall; but after tasting it, he refused to drink it. 35 When they had crucified him, they divided up his clothes by casting lots. 36 And sitting down, they kept watch over him there. 37 Above his head they placed the written charge against him: THIS IS JESUS, THE KING OF THE JEWS. 38 Two robbers were crucified with him, one on his right and one on his left. 39 Those who passed by hurled insults at him, shaking their heads 40 and saying, "You who are going to destroy the temple and build it in three days, save yourself! Come down from the cross, if you are the Son of God!" 41 In the same way the chief priests, the teachers of the law and the elders mocked him. 42 "He saved others," they said, "but he can't save himself! He's the King of Israel! Let him come down now from the cross, and we will believe in him. 43 He trusts in God. Let God rescue him now if he wants him, for he said, 'I am the Son of God.'" 44 In the same way the robbers who were crucified with him also heaped insults on him. 45 From the sixth hour until the ninth hour darkness came over all the land. 46 About

the ninth hour Jesus cried out in a loud voice, "Eloi, Eloi, lama sabachthani?"—which means, "My God, my God, why have you forsaken me?" 47 When some of those standing there heard this, they said, "He's calling Elijah." 48 Immediately one of them ran and got a sponge. He filled it with wine vinegar, put it on a stick, and offered it to Jesus to drink. 49 The rest said, "Now leave him alone. Let's see if Elijah comes to save him."

50 And when Jesus had cried out again in a loud voice, he gave up his spirit. 51 At that moment the curtain of the temple was torn in two from top to bottom. The earth shook and the rocks split. 52 The tombs broke open and the bodies of many holy people who had died were raised to life. 53 They came out of the tombs, and after Jesus' resurrection they went into the holy city and appeared to many people. 54 When the centurion and those with him who were guarding Jesus saw the earthquake and all that had happened, they were terrified, and exclaimed, "Surely he was the Son of God!" 55 Many women were there, watching from a distance. They had followed Jesus from Galilee to care for his needs. 56 Among them were Mary Magdalene, Mary the mother of James and Joses, and the mother of Zebedee's sons.

57 As evening approached, there came a rich man from Arimathea, named Joseph, who had himself become a disciple of Jesus. 58 Going to Pilate, he asked for Jesus' body, and Pilate ordered that it be given to him. 59 Joseph took the body, wrapped it in a clean linen cloth, 60 and placed it in his own new tomb that he had cut out of the rock. He rolled a big stone in front of the entrance to the tomb and went away. 61 Mary Magdalene and the other Mary were sitting there opposite the tomb. 62 The next day, the one after Preparation Day, the chief priests and the Pharisees went to Pilate. 63 "Sir," they said, "we remember that while he was still alive that deceiver said, 'After three days I will rise again. 64 So give the order for the tomb to be made secure until the third day. Otherwise, his disciples may come and steal the body and tell the people that he has been raised from the dead.

This last deception will be worse than the first." 65 "Take a guard," Pilate answered. "Go, make the tomb as secure as you know how." 66 So they went and made the tomb secure by putting a seal on the stone and posting the guard.

Matthew 28

1 After the Sabbath, at dawn on the first day of the week, Mary Magdalene and the other Mary went to look at the tomb. 2 There was a violent earthquake, for an angel of the Lord came down from heaven and, going to the tomb, rolled back the stone and sat on it. 3 His appearance was like lightning, and his clothes were white as snow. 4 The guards were so afraid of him that they shook and became like dead men. 5 The angel said to the women, "Do not be afraid, for I know that you are looking for Jesus, who was crucified. 6 He is not here; he has risen, just as he said. Come and see the place where he lay. 7 Then go quickly and tell his disciples: 'He has risen from the dead and is going ahead of you into Galilee. There you will see him.' Now I have told you." 8 So the women hurried away from the tomb, afraid yet filled with joy, and ran to tell his disciples. 9 Suddenly Jesus met them. "Greetings," he said. They came to him, clasped his feet and worshipped him. 10 Then Jesus said to them, "Do not be afraid. Go and tell my brothers to go to Galilee; there they will see me."

11 While the women were on their way, some of the guards went into the city and reported to the chief priests everything that had happened. 12 When the chief priests had met with the elders and devised a plan, they gave the soldiers a large sum of money, 13 telling them, "You are to say, 'His disciples came during the night and stole him away while we were asleep.' 14 If this report gets to the governor, we will satisfy him and keep you out of trouble." 15 So the soldiers took the money and did as they were instructed. And this story has been widely circulated among the Jews to this very day.

16 Then the eleven disciples went to Galilee, to the mountain where

Jesus had told them to go. 17 When they saw him, they worshipped him; but some doubted. 18 Then Jesus came to them and said, "All authority in heaven and on earth has been given to me. 19 Therefore go and make disciples of all nations, baptising them in the name of the Father and of the Son and of the Holy Spirit, 20 and teaching them to obey everything I have commanded you. And surely I am with you always, to the very end of the age."

Mark 15

6 Now it was the custom at the Feast to release a prisoner whom the people requested. 7 A man called Barabbas was in prison with the insurrectionists who had committed murder in the uprising. 8 The crowd came up and asked Pilate to do for them what he usually did. 9 "Do you want me to release to you the king of the Jews?" asked Pilate, 10 knowing it was out of envy that the chief priests had handed Jesus over to him. 11 But the chief priests stirred up the crowd to have Pilate release Barabbas instead. 12 "What shall I do, then, with the one you call the king of the Jews?" Pilate asked them. 13 "Crucify him!" they shouted. 14 "Why? What crime has he committed?" asked Pilate. But they shouted all the louder, "Crucify him!"

15 Wanting to satisfy the crowd, Pilate released Barabbas to them. He had Jesus flogged, and handed him over to be crucified. 16 The soldiers led Jesus away into the palace (that is, the Praetorium) and called together the whole company of soldiers. 17 They put a purple robe on him, then twisted together a crown of thorns and set it on him. 18 And they began to call out to him, "Hail, king of the Jews!" 19 Again and again they struck him on the head with a staff and spat on him. Falling on their knees, they paid homage to him. 20 And when they had mocked him, they took off the purple robe and put his own clothes on him. Then they led him out to crucify him. 21 A certain man from Cyrene, Simon, the father of Alexander and Rufus, was passing by on his way in from the country, and they forced him to carry the cross.

22 They brought Jesus to the place called Golgotha (which means The Place of the Skull). 23 Then they offered him wine mixed with myrrh, but he did not take it. 24 And they crucified him. Dividing up his clothes, they cast lots to see what each would get. 25 It was the third hour when they crucified him. 26 The written notice of the charge against him read: THE KING OF THE JEWS. 27 They crucified two robbers with him, one on his right and one on his left.

28

29 Those who passed by hurled insults at him, shaking their heads and saying, "So! You who are going to destroy the temple and build it in three days, 30 come down from the cross and save yourself!" 31 In the same way the chief priests and the teachers of the law mocked him among themselves. "He saved others," they said, "but he can't save himself! 32 Let this Christ, this King of Israel, come down now from the cross, that we may see and believe." Those crucified with him also heaped insults on him.

33 At the sixth hour darkness came over the whole land until the ninth hour. 34 And at the ninth hour Jesus cried out in a loud voice, "Eloi, Eloi, lama sabachthani?"—which means, "My God, my God, why have you forsaken me?" 35 When some of those standing near heard this, they said, "Listen, he's calling Elijah." 36 One man ran, filled a sponge with wine vinegar, put it on a stick, and offered it to Jesus to drink. "Now leave him alone. Let's see if Elijah comes to take him down," he said. 37 With a loud cry, Jesus breathed his last. 38 The curtain of the temple was torn in two from top to bottom. 39 And when the centurion, who stood there in front of Jesus, heard his cry and saw how he died, he said, "Surely this man was the Son of God!" 40 Some women were watching from a distance. Among them were Mary Magdalene, Mary the mother of James the younger and of Joses, and Salome. 41 In Galilee these women had followed him and cared for his needs. Many other women who had come up with him to Jerusalem were also there.

42 It was Preparation Day (that is, the day before the Sabbath). So as

evening approached, 43 Joseph of Arimathea, a prominent member of the Council, who was himself waiting for the kingdom of God, went boldly to Pilate and asked for Jesus' body. 44 Pilate was surprised to hear that he was already dead. Summoning the centurion, he asked him if Jesus had already died. 45 When he learned from the centurion that it was so, he gave the body to Joseph. 46 So Joseph bought some linen cloth, took down the body, wrapped it in the linen, and placed it in a tomb cut out of rock. Then he rolled a stone against the entrance of the tomb. 47 Mary Magdalene and Mary the mother of Joses saw where he was laid.

Mark 16

1 When the Sabbath was over, Mary Magdalene, Mary the mother of James, and Salome bought spices so that they might go to anoint Jesus' body. 2 Very early on the first day of the week, just after sunrise, they were on their way to the tomb 3 and they asked each other, "Who will roll the stone away from the entrance of the tomb?" 4 But when they looked up, they saw that the stone, which was very large, had been rolled away. 5 As they entered the tomb, they saw a young man dressed in a white robe sitting on the right side, and they were alarmed. 6 "Don't be alarmed," he said. "You are looking for Jesus the Nazarene, who was crucified. He has risen! He is not here. See the place where they laid him. 7 But go, tell his disciples and Peter, 'He is going ahead of you into Galilee. There you will see him, just as he told you.'" 8 Trembling and bewildered, the women went out and fled from the tomb. They said nothing to anyone, because they were afraid.

9 When Jesus rose early on the first day of the week, he appeared first to Mary Magdalene, out of whom he had driven seven demons. 10 She went and told those who had been with him and who were mourning and weeping. 11 When they heard that Jesus was alive and that she had seen him, they did not believe it. 12 Afterwards Jesus appeared in a different

form to two of them while they were walking in the country. 13 These returned and reported it to the rest; but they did not believe them either.

14 Later Jesus appeared to the Eleven as they were eating; he rebuked them for their lack of faith and their stubborn refusal to believe those who had seen him after he had risen. 15 He said to them, "Go into all the world and preach the good news to all creation. 16 Whoever believes and is baptised will be saved, but whoever does not believe will be condemned. 17 And these signs will accompany those who believe: In my name they will drive out demons; they will speak in new tongues; 18 they will pick up snakes with their hands; and when they drink deadly poison, it will not hurt them at all; they will place their hands on sick people, and they will get well."

19 After the Lord Jesus had spoken to them, he was taken up into heaven and he sat at the right hand of God. 20 Then the disciples went out and preached everywhere, and the Lord worked with them and confirmed his word by the signs that accompanied it.

Luke 22

31 "Simon, Simon, Satan has asked to sift you as wheat. 32 But I have prayed for you, Simon, that your faith may not fail. And when you have turned back, strengthen your brothers." 33 But he replied, "Lord, I am ready to go with you to prison and to death." 34 Jesus answered, "I tell you, Peter, before the cock crows today, you will deny three times that you know me." 35 Then Jesus asked them, "When I sent you without purse, bag or sandals, did you lack anything?" "Nothing," they answered. 36 He said to them, "But now if you have a purse, take it, and also a bag; and if you don't have a sword, sell your cloak and buy one. 37 It is written: 'And he was numbered with the transgressors'; and I tell you that this must be fulfilled in me. Yes, what is written about me is reaching its fulfilment." 38 The disciples said, "See, Lord, here are two swords." "That is enough," he replied.

39 Jesus went out as usual to the Mount of Olives, and his disciples followed him. 40 On reaching the place, he said to them, "Pray that you will not fall into temptation." 41 He withdrew about a stone's throw beyond them, knelt down and prayed, 42 "Father, if you are willing, take this cup from me; yet not my will, but yours be done." 43 An angel from heaven appeared to him and strengthened him. 44 And being in anguish, he prayed more earnestly, and his sweat was like drops of blood falling to the ground. 45 When he rose from prayer and went back to the disciples, he found them asleep, exhausted from sorrow. 46 "Why are you sleeping?" he asked them. "Get up and pray so that you will not fall into temptation." 47 While he was still speaking a crowd came up, and the man who was called Judas, one of the Twelve, was leading them. He approached Jesus to kiss him, 48 but Jesus asked him, "Judas, are you betraying the Son of Man with a kiss?" 49 When Jesus' followers saw what was going to happen, they said, "Lord, should we strike with our swords?" 50 And one of them struck the servant of the high priest, cutting off his right ear. 51 But Jesus answered, "No more of this!" And he touched the man's ear and healed him. 52 Then Jesus said to the chief priests, the officers of the temple guard, and the elders, who had come for him, "Am I leading a rebellion, that you have come with swords and clubs? 53 Every day I was with you in the temple courts, and you did not lay a hand on me. But this is your hour—when darkness reigns."

54 Then seizing him, they led him away and took him into the house of the high priest. Peter followed at a distance. 55 But when they had kindled a fire in the middle of the courtyard and had sat down together, Peter sat down with them. 56 A servant girl saw him seated there in the firelight. She looked closely at him and said, "This man was with him." 57 But he denied it. "Woman, I don't know him," he said. 58 A little later someone else saw him and said, "You also are one of them." "Man, I am not!" Peter replied. 59 About an hour later another asserted, "Certainly this fellow was with him, for he is a Galilean." 60 Peter replied, "Man, I don't

know what you're talking about!" Just as he was speaking, the cock crowed. 61 The Lord turned and looked straight at Peter. Then Peter remembered the word the Lord had spoken to him: "Before the cock crows today, you will disown me three times." 62 And he went outside and wept bitterly.

63 The men who were guarding Jesus began mocking and beating him. 64 They blindfolded him and demanded, "Prophesy! Who hit you?" 65 And they said many other insulting things to him. 66 At daybreak the council of the elders of the people, both the chief priests and teachers of the law, met together, and Jesus was led before them. 67 "If you are the Christ," they said, "tell us." Jesus answered, "If I tell you, you will not believe me, 68 and if I asked you, you would not answer. 69 But from now on, the Son of Man will be seated at the right hand of the mighty God." 70 They all asked, "Are you then the Son of God?" He replied, "You are right in saying I am." 71 Then they said, "Why do we need any more testimony? We have heard it from his own lips."

Luke 23

1 Then the whole assembly rose and led him off to Pilate. 2 And they began to accuse him, saying, "We have found this man subverting our nation. He opposes payment of taxes to Caesar and claims to be Christ, a king." 3 So Pilate asked Jesus, "Are you the king of the Jews?" "Yes, it is as you say," Jesus replied. 4 Then Pilate announced to the chief priests and the crowd, "I find no basis for a charge against this man." 5 But they insisted, "He stirs up the people all over Judea by his teaching. He started in Galilee and has come all the way here." 6 On hearing this, Pilate asked if the man was a Galilean. 7 When he learned that Jesus was under Herod's jurisdiction, he sent him to Herod, who was also in Jerusalem at that time. 8 When Herod saw Jesus, he was greatly pleased, because for a long time he had been wanting to see him. From what he had heard about him, he hoped to see him perform some miracle. 9 He plied him with many questions, but Jesus

gave him no answer. 10 The chief priests and the teachers of the law were standing there, vehemently accusing him. 11 Then Herod and his soldiers ridiculed and mocked him. Dressing him in an elegant robe, they sent him back to Pilate. 12 That day Herod and Pilate became friends—before this they had been enemies.

13 Pilate called together the chief priests, the rulers and the people, 14 and said to them, "You brought me this man as one who was inciting the people to rebellion. I have examined him in your presence and have found no basis for your charges against him. 15 Neither has Herod, for he sent him back to us; as you can see, he has done nothing to deserve death. 16 Therefore, I will punish him and then release him." 17 18 With one voice they cried out, "Away with this man! Release Barabbas to us!" 19 (Barabbas had been thrown into prison for an insurrection in the city, and for murder.) 20 Wanting to release Jesus, Pilate appealed to them again. 21 But they kept shouting, "Crucify him! Crucify him!" 22 For the third time he spoke to them: "Why? What crime has this man committed? I have found in him no grounds for the death penalty. Therefore I will have him punished and then release him." 23 But with loud shouts they insistently demanded that he be crucified, and their shouts prevailed.24 So Pilate decided to grant their demand. 25 He released the man who had been thrown into prison for insurrection and murder, the one they asked for, and surrendered Jesus to their will.

26 As they led him away, they seized Simon from Cyrene, who was on his way in from the country, and put the cross on him and made him carry it behind Jesus. 27 A large number of people followed him, including women who mourned and wailed for him. 28 Jesus turned and said to them, "Daughters of Jerusalem, do not weep for me; weep for yourselves and for your children. 29 For the time will come when you will say, 'Blessed are the barren women, the wombs that never bore and the breasts that never nursed!' 30 Then "'they will say to the mountains, "Fall on

us!" and to the hills "Cover us!"' 31 For if men do these things when the tree is green, what will happen when it is dry?"

32 Two other men, both criminals, were also led out with him to be executed. 33 When they came to the place called the Skull, there they crucified him, along with the criminals—one on his right, the other on his left. 34 Jesus said, "Father, forgive them, for they do not know what they are doing." And they divided up his clothes by casting lots. 35 The people stood watching, and the rulers even sneered at him. They said, "He saved others; let him save himself if he is the Christ of God, the Chosen One." 36 The soldiers also came up and mocked him. They offered him wine vinegar 37 and said, "If you are the king of the Jews, save yourself." 38 There was a written notice above him, which read: THIS IS THE KING OF THE JEWS. 39 One of the criminals who hung there hurled insults at him: "Aren't you the Christ? Save yourself and us!" 40 But the other criminal rebuked him. "Don't you fear God," he said, "since you are under the same sentence? 41 We are punished justly, for we are getting what our deeds deserve. But this man has done nothing wrong." 42 Then he said, "Jesus, remember me when you come into your kingdom." 43 Jesus answered him, "I tell you the truth, today you will be with me in paradise."

44 It was now about the sixth hour, and darkness came over the whole land until the ninth hour, 45 for the sun stopped shining. And the curtain of the temple was torn in two. 46 Jesus called out with a loud voice, "Father, into your hands I commit my spirit." When he had said this, he breathed his last. 47 The centurion, seeing what had happened, praised God and said, "Surely this was a righteous man." 48 When all the people who had gathered to witness this sight saw what took place, they beat their breasts and went away. 49 But all those who knew him, including the women who had followed him from Galilee, stood at a distance, watching these things.

50 Now there was a man named Joseph, a member of the Council, a good

and upright man, 51 who had not consented to their decision and action. He came from the Judean town of Arimathea and he was waiting for the kingdom of God. 52 Going to Pilate, he asked for Jesus' body. 53 Then he took it down, wrapped it in linen cloth and placed it in a tomb cut in the rock, one in which no-one had yet been laid. 54 It was Preparation Day, and the Sabbath was about to begin. 55 The women who had come with Jesus from Galilee followed Joseph and saw the tomb and how his body was laid in it. 56 Then they went home and prepared spices and perfumes. But they rested on the Sabbath in obedience to the commandment.

Luke 24

1 On the first day of the week, very early in the morning, the women took the spices they had prepared and went to the tomb. 2 They found the stone rolled away from the tomb, 3 but when they entered, they did not find the body of the Lord Jesus. 4 While they were wondering about this, suddenly two men in clothes that gleamed like lightning stood beside them. 5 In their fright the women bowed down with their faces to the ground, but the men said to them, "Why do you look for the living among the dead? 6 He is not here; he has risen! Remember how he told you, while he was still with you in Galilee: 7 'The Son of Man must be delivered into the hands of sinful men, be crucified and on the third day be raised again.'" 8 Then they remembered his words. 9 When they came back from the tomb, they told all these things to the Eleven and to all the others. 10 It was Mary Magdalene, Joanna, Mary the mother of James, and the others with them who told this to the apostles. 11 But they did not believe the women, because their words seemed to them like nonsense. 12 Peter, however, got up and ran to the tomb. Bending over, he saw the strips of linen lying by themselves, and he went away, wondering to himself what had happened.

13 Now that same day two of them were going to a village called Emmaus, about seven miles from Jerusalem. 14 They were talking with

each other about everything that had happened. 15 As they talked and discussed these things with each other, Jesus himself came up and walked along with them; 16 but they were kept from recognising him. 17 He asked them, "What are you discussing together as you walk along?" They stood still, their faces downcast. 18 One of them, named Cleopas, asked him, "Are you only a visitor to Jerusalem and do not know the things that have happened there in these days?" 19 "What things?" he asked. "About Jesus of Nazareth," they replied. "He was a prophet, powerful in word and deed before God and all the people. 20 The chief priests and our rulers handed him over to be sentenced to death, and they crucified him; 21 but we had hoped that he was the one who was going to redeem Israel. And what is more, it is the third day since all this took place. 22 In addition, some of our women amazed us. They went to the tomb early this morning 23 but didn't find his body. They came and told us that they had seen a vision of angels, who said he was alive. 24 Then some of our companions went to the tomb and found it just as the women had said, but him they did not see." 25 He said to them, "How foolish you are, and how slow of heart to believe all that the prophets have spoken! 26 Did not the Christ have to suffer these things and then enter his glory?" 27 And beginning with Moses and all the Prophets, he explained to them what was said in all the Scriptures concerning himself. 28 As they approached the village to which they were going, Jesus acted as if he were going further. 29 But they urged him strongly, "Stay with us, for it is nearly evening; the day is almost over." So he went in to stay with them. 30 When he was at the table with them, he took bread, gave thanks, broke it and began to give it to them. 31 Then their eyes were opened and they recognised him, and he disappeared from their sight. 32 They asked each other, "Were not our hearts burning within us while he talked with us on the road and opened the Scriptures to us?" 33 They got up and returned at once to Jerusalem. There they found the Eleven and those with them, assembled together 34 and saying, "It is true! The Lord has risen and has appeared to Simon." 35 Then the two told what had happened on the way, and how Jesus was recognised by them when he broke the bread.

36 While they were still talking about this, Jesus himself stood among them and said to them, "Peace be with you." 37 They were startled and frightened, thinking they saw a ghost. 38 He said to them, "Why are you troubled, and why do doubts rise in your minds? 39 Look at my hands and my feet. It is I myself! Touch me and see; a ghost does not have flesh and bones, as you see I have." 40 When he had said this, he showed them his hands and feet. 41 And while they still did not believe it because of joy and amazement, he asked them, "Do you have anything here to eat?" 42 They gave him a piece of broiled fish, 43 and he took it and ate it in their presence. 44 He said to them, "This is what I told you while I was still with you: Everything must be fulfilled that is written about me in the Law of Moses, the Prophets and the Psalms." 45 Then he opened their minds so they could understand the Scriptures. 46 He told them, "This is what is written: The Christ will suffer and rise from the dead on the third day, 47 and repentance and forgiveness of sins will be preached in his name to all nations, beginning at Jerusalem. 48 You are witnesses of these things. 49 I am going to send you what my Father has promised; but stay in the city until you have been clothed with power from on high."

50 When he had led them out to the vicinity of Bethany, he lifted up his hands and blessed them. 51 While he was blessing them, he left them and was taken up into heaven. 52 Then they worshipped him and returned to Jerusalem with great joy. 53 And they stayed continually at the temple, praising God.

John 18

28 Then the Jews led Jesus from Caiaphas to the palace of the Roman governor. By now it was early morning, and to avoid ceremonial uncleanness the Jews did not enter the palace; they wanted to be able to eat the Passover. 29 So Pilate came out to them and asked, "What charges are

you bringing against this man?" 30 "If he were not a criminal," they replied, "we would not have handed him over to you." 31 Pilate said, "Take him yourselves and judge him by your own law." "But we have no right to execute anyone," the Jews objected. 32 This happened so that the words Jesus had spoken indicating the kind of death he was going to die would be fulfilled. 33 Pilate then went back inside the palace, summoned Jesus and asked him, "Are you the king of the Jews?" 34 "Is that your own idea," Jesus asked, "or did others talk to you about me?" 35 "Am I a Jew?" Pilate replied. "It was your people and your chief priests who handed you over to me. What is it you have done?" 36 Jesus said, "My kingdom is not of this world. If it were, my servants would fight to prevent my arrest by the Jews. But now my kingdom is from another place." 37 "You are a king, then!" said Pilate. Jesus answered, "You are right in saying I am a king. In fact, for this reason I was born, and for this I came into the world, to testify to the truth. Everyone on the side of truth listens to me." 38 "What is truth?" Pilate asked. With this he went out again to the Jews and said, "I find no basis for a charge against him. 39 But it is your custom for me to release to you one prisoner at the time of the Passover. Do you want me to release 'the king of the Jews'?" 40 They shouted back, "No, not him! Give us Barabbas!" Now Barabbas had taken part in a rebellion.

John 19

1 Then Pilate took Jesus and had him flogged. 2 The soldiers twisted together a crown of thorns and put it on his head. They clothed him in a purple robe 3 and went up to him again and again, saying, "Hail, king of the Jews!" And they struck him in the face. 4 Once more Pilate came out and said to the Jews, "Look, I am bringing him out to you to let you know that I find no basis for a charge against him." 5 When Jesus came out wearing the crown of thorns and the purple robe, Pilate said to them, "Here is the man!" 6 As soon as the chief priests and their officials saw him, they shouted, "Crucify! Crucify!" But Pilate answered, "You take

him and crucify him. As for me, I find no basis for a charge against him." 7 The Jews insisted, "We have a law, and according to that law he must die, because he claimed to be the Son of God." 8 When Pilate heard this, he was even more afraid, 9 and he went back inside the palace. "Where do you come from?" he asked Jesus, but Jesus gave him no answer. 10 "Do you refuse to speak to me?" Pilate said. "Don't you realise I have power either to free you or to crucify you?" 11 Jesus answered, "You would have no power over me if it were not given to you from above. Therefore the one who handed me over to you is guilty of a greater sin." 12 From then on, Pilate tried to set Jesus free, but the Jews kept shouting, "If you let this man go, you are no friend of Caesar. Anyone who claims to be a king opposes Caesar." 13 When Pilate heard this, he brought Jesus out and sat down on the judge's seat at a place known as the Stone Pavement (which in Aramaic is Gabbatha). 14 It was the day of Preparation of Passover Week, about the sixth hour. "Here is your king," Pilate said to the Jews. 15 But they shouted, "Take him away! Take him away! Crucify him!" "Shall I crucify your king?" Pilate asked. "We have no king but Caesar," the chief priests answered.

16 Finally Pilate handed him over to them to be crucified. So the soldiers took charge of Jesus. 17 Carrying his own cross, he went out to the place of the Skull (which in Aramaic is called Golgotha). 18 Here they crucified him, and with him two others—one on each side and Jesus in the middle.

19 Pilate had a notice prepared and fastened to the cross. It read: JESUS OF NAZARETH, THE KING OF THE JEWS. 20 Many of the Jews read this sign, for the place where Jesus was crucified was near the city, and the sign was written in Aramaic, Latin and Greek. 21 The chief priests of the Jews protested to Pilate, "Do not write 'The King of the Jews', but that this man claimed to be king of the Jews." 22 Pilate answered, "What I have written, I have written." 23 When the soldiers crucified Jesus, they took his clothes, dividing them into four shares, one for each of them, with the

undergarment remaining. This garment was seamless, woven in one piece from top to bottom. 24 "Let's not tear it," they said to one another. "Let's decide by lot who will get it." This happened that the scripture might be fulfilled which said, "They divided my garments among them and cast lots for my clothing." So this is what the soldiers did. 25 Near the cross of Jesus stood his mother, his mother's sister, Mary the wife of Clopas, and Mary Magdalene. 26 When Jesus saw his mother there, and the disciple whom he loved standing near by, he said to his mother, "Dear woman, here is your son," 27 and to the disciple, "Here is your mother." From that time on, this disciple took her into his home. 28 Later, knowing that all was now completed, and so that the Scripture would be fulfilled, Jesus said, "I am thirsty." 29 A jar of wine vinegar was there, so they soaked a sponge in it, put the sponge on a stalk of the hyssop plant, and lifted it to Jesus' lips. 30 When he had received the drink, Jesus said, "It is finished." With that, he bowed his head and gave up his spirit.

31 Now it was the day of Preparation, and the next day was to be a special Sabbath. Because the Jews did not want the bodies left on the crosses during the Sabbath, they asked Pilate to have the legs broken and the bodies taken down. 32 The soldiers therefore came and broke the legs of the first man who had been crucified with Jesus, and then those of the other. 33 But when they came to Jesus and found that he was already dead, they did not break his legs. 34 Instead, one of the soldiers pierced Jesus' side with a spear, bringing a sudden flow of blood and water. 35 The man who saw it has given testimony, and his testimony is true. He knows that he tells the truth, and he testifies so that you also may believe. 36 These things happened so that the scripture would be fulfilled: "Not one of his bones will be broken," 37 and, as another scripture says, "They will look on the one they have pierced."

38 Later, Joseph of Arimathea asked Pilate for the body of Jesus. Now Joseph was a disciple of Jesus, but secretly because he feared the Jews. With Pilate's permission, he came and took the body away. 39 He was

accompanied by Nicodemus, the man who earlier had visited Jesus at night. Nicodemus brought a mixture of myrrh and aloes, about seventy-five pounds. 40 Taking Jesus' body, the two of them wrapped it, with the spices, in strips of linen. This was in accordance with Jewish burial customs. 41 At the place where Jesus was crucified, there was a garden, and in the garden a new tomb, in which no-one had ever been laid. 42 Because it was the Jewish day of Preparation and since the tomb was near by, they laid Jesus there.

John 20

1 Early on the first day of the week, while it was still dark, Mary Magdalene went to the tomb and saw that the stone had been removed from the entrance. 2 So she came running to Simon Peter and the other disciple, the one Jesus loved, and said, "They have taken the Lord out of the tomb, and we don't know where they have put him!" 3 So Peter and the other disciple started for the tomb. 4 Both were running, but the other disciple outran Peter and reached the tomb first. 5 He bent over and looked in at the strips of linen lying there but did not go in. 6 Then Simon Peter, who was behind him, arrived and went into the tomb. He saw the strips of linen lying there, 7 as well as the burial cloth that had been around Jesus' head. The cloth was folded up by itself, separate from the linen. 8 Finally the other disciple, who had reached the tomb first, also went inside. He saw and believed. 9 (They still did not understand from Scripture that Jesus had to rise from the dead.) 10 Then the disciples went back to their homes,

11 but Mary stood outside the tomb crying. As she wept, she bent over to look into the tomb 12 and saw two angels in white, seated where Jesus' body had been, one at the head and the other at the foot. 13 They asked her, "Woman, why are you crying?" "They have taken my Lord away," she said, "and I don't know where they have put him." 14 At this, she turned round and saw Jesus standing there, but she did not realise that it was Jesus.

15 "Woman," he said, "why are you crying? Who is it you are looking for?" Thinking he was the gardener, she said, "Sir, if you have carried him away, tell me where you have put him, and I will get him." 16 Jesus said to her, "Mary." She turned towards him and cried out in Aramaic, "Rabboni!" (which means Teacher). 17 Jesus said, "Do not hold on to me, for I have not yet returned to the Father. Go instead to my brothers and tell them, 'I am returning to my Father and your Father, to my God and your God.'" 18 Mary Magdalene went to the disciples with the news: "I have seen the Lord!" And she told them that he had said these things to her.

19 On the evening of that first day of the week, when the disciples were together, with the doors locked for fear of the Jews, Jesus came and stood among them and said, "Peace be with you!" 20 After he said this, he showed them his hands and side. The disciples were overjoyed when they saw the Lord. 21 Again Jesus said, "Peace be with you! As the Father has sent me, I am sending you." 22 And with that he breathed on them and said, "Receive the Holy Spirit. 23 If you forgive anyone his sins, they are forgiven; if you do not forgive them, they are not forgiven." 24 Now Thomas (called Didymus), one of the Twelve, was not with the disciples when Jesus came. 25 So the other disciples told him, "We have seen the Lord!" But he said to them, "Unless I see the nail marks in his hands and put my finger where the nails were, and put my hand into his side, I will not believe it."

26 A week later his disciples were in the house again, and Thomas was with them. Though the doors were locked, Jesus came and stood among them and said, "Peace be with you!" 27 Then he said to Thomas, "Put your finger here; see my hands. Reach out your hand and put it into my side. Stop doubting and believe." 28 Thomas said to him, "My Lord and my God!" 29 Then Jesus told him, "Because you have seen me, you have believed; blessed are those who have not seen and yet have believed." 30 Jesus did many other miraculous signs in the presence of his disciples, which are not recorded in this book. 31 But these are

written that you may believe that Jesus is the Christ, the Son of God, and that by believing you may have life in his name.

John 21

1 Afterwards Jesus appeared again to his disciples, by the Sea of Tiberias. It happened this way: 2 Simon Peter, Thomas (called Didymus), Nathanael from Cana in Galilee, the sons of Zebedee, and two other disciples were together. 3 "I'm going out to fish," Simon Peter told them, and they said, "We'll go with you." So they went out and got into the boat, but that night they caught nothing. 4 Early in the morning, Jesus stood on the shore, but the disciples did not realise that it was Jesus. 5 He called out to them, "Friends, haven't you any fish?" "No," they answered. 6 He said, "Throw your net on the right side of the boat and you will find some." When they did, they were unable to haul the net in because of the large number of fish. 7 Then the disciple whom Jesus loved said to Peter, "It is the Lord!" As soon as Simon Peter heard him say, "It is the Lord," he wrapped his outer garment around him (for he had taken it off) and jumped into the water. 8 The other disciples followed in the boat, towing the net full of fish, for they were not far from shore, about a hundred yards. 9 When they landed, they saw a fire of burning coals there with fish on it, and some bread. 10 Jesus said to them, "Bring some of the fish you have just caught." 11 Simon Peter climbed aboard and dragged the net ashore. It was full of large fish, 153, but even with so many the net was not torn. 12 Jesus said to them, "Come and have breakfast." None of the disciples dared ask him, "Who are you?" They knew it was the Lord. 13 Jesus came, took the bread and gave it to them, and did the same with the fish. 14 This was now the third time Jesus appeared to his disciples after he was raised from the dead.

15 When they had finished eating, Jesus said to Simon Peter, "Simon son of John, do you truly love me more than these?" "Yes, Lord," he said, "you know that I love you." Jesus said, "Feed my lambs." 16 Again Jesus said, "Simon son of John, do you truly love me?" He answered, "Yes, Lord, you

know that I love you." Jesus said, "Take care of my sheep." 17 The third time he said to him, "Simon son of John, do you love me?" Peter was hurt because Jesus asked him the third time, "Do you love me?" He said, "Lord, you know all things; you know that I love you." Jesus said, "Feed my sheep. 18 I tell you the truth, when you were younger you dressed yourself and went where you wanted; but when you are old you will stretch out your hands, and someone else will dress you and lead you where you do not want to go." 19 Jesus said this to indicate the kind of death by which Peter would glorify God. Then he said to him, "Follow me!"

20 Peter turned and saw that the disciple whom Jesus loved was following them. (This was the one who had leaned back against Jesus at the supper and had said, "Lord, who is going to betray you?") 21 When Peter saw him, he asked, "Lord, what about him?" 22 Jesus answered, "If I want him to remain alive until I return, what is that to you? You must follow me." 23 Because of this, the rumour spread among the brothers that this disciple would not die. But Jesus did not say that he would not die; he only said, "If I want him to remain alive until I return, what is that to you?" 24 This is the disciple who testifies to these things and who wrote them down. We know that his testimony is true. 25 Jesus did many other things as well. If every one of them were written down, I suppose that even the whole world would not have room for the books that would be written.

Acts 26

1 Then Agrippa said to Paul, "You have permission to speak for yourself." So Paul motioned with his hand and began his defence: 2 "King Agrippa, I consider myself fortunate to stand before you today as I make my defence against all the accusations of the Jews, 3 and especially so because you are well acquainted with all the Jewish customs and controversies. Therefore, I beg you to listen to me patiently. 4 "The Jews all know the way I have lived ever since I was a child, from the beginning of my life in

my own country, and also in Jerusalem. 5 They have known me for a long time and can testify, if they are willing, that according to the strictest sect of our religion, I lived as a Pharisee. 6 And now it is because of my hope in what God has promised our fathers that I am on trial today. 7 This is the promise our twelve tribes are hoping to see fulfilled as they earnestly serve God day and night. O King, it is because of this hope that the Jews are accusing me. 8 Why should any of you consider it incredible that God raises the dead? 9 "I too was convinced that I ought to do all that was possible to oppose the name of Jesus of Nazareth. 10 And that is just what I did in Jerusalem. On the authority of the chief priests I put many of the saints in prison, and when they were put to death, I cast my vote against them. 11 Many a time I went from one synagogue to another to have them punished, and I tried to force them to blaspheme. In my obsession against them, I even went to foreign cities to persecute them.

12 "On one of these journeys I was going to Damascus with the authority and commission of the chief priests. 13 About noon, O King, as I was on the road, I saw a light from heaven, brighter than the sun, blazing around me and my companions. 14 We all fell to the ground, and I heard a voice saying to me in Aramaic, 'Saul, Saul, why do you persecute me? It is hard for you to kick against the goads.' 15 "Then I asked, 'Who are you, Lord?' "'I am Jesus, whom you are persecuting,' the Lord replied. 16 'Now get up and stand on your feet. I have appeared to you to appoint you as a servant and as a witness of what you have seen of me and what I will show you. 17 I will rescue you from your own people and from the Gentiles. I am sending you to them 18 to open their eyes and turn them from darkness to light, and from the power of Satan to God, so that they may receive forgiveness of sins and a place among those who are sanctified by faith in me.' 19 "So then, King Agrippa, I was not disobedient to the vision from heaven. 20 First to those in Damascus, then to those in Jerusalem and in all Judea, and to the Gentiles also, I preached that they should repent and turn to God and prove their repentance by their deeds. 21 That is why the Jews seized me in the temple courts and tried to kill

me. 22 But I have had God's help to this very day, and so I stand here and testify to small and great alike. I am saying nothing beyond what the prophets and Moses said would happen—23 that the Christ would suffer and, as the first to rise from the dead, would proclaim light to his own people and to the Gentiles."

Romans 14

7 For none of us lives to himself alone and none of us dies to himself alone. 8 If we live, we live to the Lord; and if we die, we die to the Lord. So, whether we live or die, we belong to the Lord. 9 For this very reason, Christ died and returned to life so that he might be the Lord of both the dead and the living.

1 Corinthians 6

19 Or do you not know that your body is the temple of the Holy Spirit *who is* in you, whom you have from God, and you are not your own? 20 For you were bought at a price; therefore glorify God in your body and in your spirit, which are God's.

1 Corinthians 15

1 Now, brothers, I want to remind you of the gospel I preached to you, which you received and on which you have taken your stand. 2 By this gospel you are saved, if you hold firmly to the word I preached to you. Otherwise, you have believed in vain. 3 For what I received I passed on to you as of first importance: that Christ died for our sins according to the Scriptures, 4 that he was buried, that he was raised on the third day according to the Scriptures, 5 and that he appeared to Peter, and then to the Twelve. 6 After that, he appeared to more than five hundred of the brothers at the same time, most of whom are still living, though some have fallen asleep. 7 Then he appeared to James, then to all the apostles, 8 and last of all he appeared to me also, as to one abnormally born. 9 For I am the least

of the apostles and do not even deserve to be called an apostle, because I persecuted the church of God. 10 But by the grace of God I am what I am, and his grace to me was not without effect. No, I worked harder than all of them yet not I, but the grace of God that was with me. 11 Whether, then, it was I or they, this is what we preach, and this is what you believed.

12 But if it is preached that Christ has been raised from the dead, how can some of you say that there is no resurrection of the dead? 13 If there is no resurrection of the dead, then not even Christ has been raised. 14 And if Christ has not been raised, our preaching is useless and so is your faith. 15 More than that, we are then found to be false witnesses about God, for we have testified about God that he raised Christ from the dead. But he did not raise him if in fact the dead are not raised. 16 For if the dead are not raised, then Christ has not been raised either. 17 And if Christ has not been raised, your faith is futile; you are still in your sins. 18 Then those also who have fallen asleep in Christ are lost. 19 If only for this life we have hope in Christ, we are to be pitied more than all men.

20 But Christ has indeed been raised from the dead, the firstfruits of those who have fallen asleep. 21 For since death came through a man, the resurrection of the dead comes also through a man. 22 For as in Adam all die, so in Christ all will be made alive.

2 Corinthians 5

14 For Christ's love compels us, because we are convinced that one died for all, and therefore all died. 15 And he died for all, that those who live should no longer live for themselves but for him who died for them and was raised again.

16 So from now on we regard no one from a worldly point of view. Though we once regarded Christ in this way, we do so no longer. 17 Therefore, if anyone is in Christ, he is a new creation; the old has gone, the new has come! 18 All this is from God, who reconciled us to himself through Christ and gave us the ministry of reconciliation: 19 that God was

reconciling the world to himself in Christ, not counting men's sins against them. And he has committed to us the message of reconciliation. 20 We are therefore Christ's ambassadors, as though God were making his appeal through us. We implore you on God's behalf: Be reconciled to God. 21 God made him who had no sin to be sin for us, so that in him we might become the righteousness of God.